LITERACY TEACHING AND LEARNING IN RURAL COMMUNITIES

"This book provides a clear and compelling window into the realities of rural teaching. The writers make it possible to imagine rural teaching as a rewarding professional career. I wish I'd had this book when I was a young teacher!"
Robert Brooke, University of Nebraska–Lincoln, USA

This definitive look at teaching English in rural secondary schools contests current definitions and discussions of rural education, examines their ideological and cultural foundations, and presents an alternative perspective that conceptualizes rural communities as diverse, unique, and conducive to pedagogical and personal growth in teaching and learning. Authentic narratives document individual teachers' moments of struggle and success in learning to understand, value, and incorporate rural literacies and sensibilities into their curricula. The teachers' stories and the scholarly analysis of issues raised through them illuminate the unique challenges and rewards of teaching English in a rural school and offer helpful insights and knowledge for navigating the pedagogical landscape.

Lisa Schade Eckert is Associate Professor of English at Northern Michigan University, USA.

Janet Alsup is Professor of English Education, Purdue University, USA.

LITERACY TEACHING AND LEARNING IN RURAL COMMUNITIES

Problematizing Stereotypes, Challenging Myths

Edited by
Lisa Schade Eckert and Janet Alsup

Routledge
Taylor & Francis Group

NEW YORK AND LONDON

First published 2015
by Routledge
711 Third Avenue, New York, NY 10017

and by Routledge
2 Park Square, Milton Park, Abingdon, Oxon OX14 4RN

Routledge is an imprint of the Taylor & Francis Group, an informa business

Library of Congress Cataloging-in-Publication Data

Literacy teaching and learning in rural communities : problematizing
    stereotypes, challenging myths / edited by Lisa S. Eckert, Northern
    Michigan University, Janet Alsup, Purdue University.
        pages cm
    Includes bibliographical references and index.
    1. Literacy—Study and teaching.   2. Literacy—Social aspects.   3. Rural
education.   I. Eckert, Lisa Schade.   II. Alsup, Janet.
    LC149.L518 2015
    302.2'244—dc23
    2014030168

ISBN: 978-1-138-82233-7 (hbk)
ISBN: 978-1-138-82234-4 (pbk)
ISBN: 978-1-315-74287-8 (ebk)

Typeset in Bembo
by Apex CoVantage, LLC

Printed and bound in the United States of America by Publishers Graphics, LLC on sustainably sourced paper.

For all the youth in American rural schools and the teachers who teach them

CONTENTS

community aspects become reflected and embraced by teachers who engage students in reading, writing, speaking, listening, and, most of all, thinking about their lives, literature, and the lives of their communities.

To conclude, I offer a hearty Brava! to the authors and editors of this volume. The readers who will take up your work and learn from it are lucky, indeed.

PREFACE

Stories are a unique and essential way of coming to know, of coming to understand self and other. Many theorists and researchers in the fields of psychology, education, and philosophy, as well as literary study, have argued for the importance of narrative in both forming and representing human identity. Jerome Bruner (1986), possibly the most famous theorist of narrative, has argued that people lead "storied lives," and that "self making is a narrative art" (p. 65). Narratology, or the "theory of narratives, narrative texts, images, spectacles, events" (Bal, 1999, p. 3) is a field of study that examines and describes all types of narratives and uses of narratives. In the 1960s and 1970s, narratology was concerned primarily with literary study and analyzing the role of narratives in texts (Booth, 1961; Campbell, 1972; Frye, 1964); more recently, interest in narrative has expanded to include sociocultural examinations of the role of narrative in identity construction, culture, and communicative contexts (Jahn, 1999; Schaafsma, Pagnucci, Wallace, and Stock, 2007).

In this book we have collected nine teacher narratives, stories written by teachers about their diverse experiences teaching in rural schools. We found these stories to be unfailingly sincere, honest, and heartfelt. Consistent with how Connelly and Clandinin (2006) define narrative inquiry, we view these teacher stories as a "way of thinking about experience" (p. 375), a way of beginning to understand the lived experience of rural teachers across the US. While we cannot call ourselves traditional empirical researchers in this project, we come to these stories in the spirit of inquiry, to learn through the narrative retellings how rural teachers understand themselves and their professional lives—so that we can better prepare young teachers who follow in their footsteps as well as inspire rural teachers currently in the classroom.

These stories from rural teachers deconstruct myths of the "rhetoric of lack" (Donehower, Hogg, and Schell, 2007) and negative prejudice of teaching/teachers in rural communities (Theobald and Wood, 2010), but do acknowledge the challenges inherent in beginning and sustaining a teaching career in a community outside of one's personal and professional experience. The challenges noted in the narratives are often a result of lack of understanding of the rural community, breadth of professional and curricular responsibilities, and the significant gap in identity development required of all teachers but specific to teachers who, because they have not had personal or professional experiences in rural educational settings via field placements or curricular materials in a teacher education program, may lack even a vicarious understanding or experience with rurality. Stories of triumph include notable success in curricular achievement, personal and professional development, development of understanding of the diversities inherent in rural communities that may initially go unnoticed (e.g., socioeconomic, linguistic, economic, popular culture, etc.), recognizing funds of knowledge (see Moll and Gonzalez, 1994, p. 443), and/or richness of place and space unique to rural communities.

As we read the submitted narratives we realized that the experiences as rural teachers differed according to the time spent in the field and years of experience as a teacher. Therefore, we organized this book into two major sections—early career rural educators, and mid- to late-career rural educators—with short introductions to contextualize and theorize each. We asked each of our contributors to describe the community and context of his or her teaching situation to define his or her own concept of rurality in schooling and communicate that situational definition with the reader. They also mention their own conflicting subjectivities as rural outsiders coming into a rural community, financial and policy restrictions often faced by small schools in rural places, and their struggles and successes learning to understand, value, and incorporate rural literacies (Donehower et al., 2007; Green and Corbett, 2013) and sensibilities into their curricula.

Chapter Summaries

Part I From Stranger to Native: Early Career Teacher Narratives

The chapters that comprise this section are written by early career teachers who describe the shock of initial identity clash between becoming and being a literacy teacher, exacerbated by their lack of familiarity and preparation for the particular rural community in which they find themselves. Each teacher confronts the realities of being a 'stranger teacher' and shares the struggle of personal and professional identity growth and change—of stepping into the role of a public intellectual in a community and way of life with which he or she is unfamiliar. They are learning how the site of one's education can be as important as its other dimensions, both to the students who are rural natives and the faculty who struggle with place-based inequities and policy challenges. Finally, these new teachers are also learning what it means to love the rural and those within it.

Chapter 3: A Rural Education: From Stranger to Strangerer

Taylor Norman writes from the perspective of a young teacher in central Indiana who is not from a rural area, yet finds herself teaching literacy in a rural high school. She struggles with her perceived conflict between her own culturally grounded opinions of the value of education and the values of her rural students. She must work through these biases to not only become a better teacher, but a teacher who understands and respects the rural values enacted by her students. In short, she must move from a place of anger to one of love.

Chapter 4: Crossing the Tracks, or The Bacon of Despair: The Story of One Teacher's Story . . . of One Teacher's Story . . . of Teaching in a Rural School

Jeff Spanke is likewise a new teacher who must rethink his before-unseen bias against rural educational sensibilities. Moving from a suburban community where most attend college and take on white-collar professions, Jeff takes a job in a small rural school in the Midwest and must deal with his frustration at their perceived otherness. Jeff grapples with his own feelings of being a stranger in a strange land by writing original fiction paralleling, and extending, his real-life experience.

Chapter 5: Falling Through the Rabbit Hole and Teaching Through the Looking Glass: Experiences of a New Teacher in a Rural School

Kendra McPheeters-Neal, another new literacy teacher in a rural school in west central Indiana, also often feels like a stranger during that first year. In fact, she compares the experience to Alice moving through the looking glass into an unfamiliar world where everything seems backwards and upside down. Like Taylor and Jeff, however, Kendra narrates her experience of coming to terms with her own cultural alienation as she confronts so-called rural issues such as the lack of resources, nonstandard language, and dated gender role expectations. Kendra, however, also realizes that the identities of rural teens are as complex and varied as those in any other setting, and the experiences of rural students (or teachers) cannot be easily essentialized or codified as 'rural.' The other side of the looking glass isn't that different after all.

Chapter 6: Is There Such a Thing as Caring Too Much? A Farm Girl Swims With Sharks

Chea Parton, the last new teacher in the collection, also struggles with outsider feelings, despite her own experience growing up in a rural area. Her story focuses on these feelings of alienation, but she also narrates how a young teacher in a rural school handles standardized assessments and policies that often affect small, rural districts, with few faculty and even fewer resources, in exaggerated ways. At the end of her second year, Chea decides to remain in her rural teaching position and continue to teach the students she has grown increasingly fond of, even though, in her own words, she sometimes feels as if she "cares too much." Chea will continue balancing the many external demands and pressures she and her school face with her reasons for becoming a teacher in the first place: to improve students' lives.

Part II Teaching Through Place: Mid- to Late-Career Teacher Narratives

The chapters that comprise this section of the book share the growth of English or literacy teachers who have taught in rural school settings for anywhere from 5 to 30 years. We found that successful teachers are able to construct an intellectual identity that is largely in harmony, or at least complimentary, with what they have come to understand about the place and community in which they are teaching. As one experienced rural teacher said: "Revered or reviled—you're intimidating and intimidated." We feel that these narratives will provide early career teachers with a model to follow, or at least a better understanding of what they can do to find balance, the means to carve out a niche, and the ultimate responsibility of assuming the role of a public intellectual within the community. The teachers describe, with humor and grace, the ways in which they learned to combine their pedagogical understandings and beliefs with what they learned about the community through their initial teaching experiences. They have learned to develop curricula which incorporate the communities' knowledge and values as a starting point for enriching community discourses without overpowering or subverting them. In short, they share the ways in which they stepped into the role and developed the identity of the public intellectual parallel to the organic concept of the community in which they live and work.

Chapter 8: Lessons From the Inside Out: Poetry, Epiphanies, and Creative Literary Culture in a Rural Montana High School

Jeffrey B. Ross describes his pedagogical and personal adjustment into the Belt community, a former coal mining town that has developed into a mix of ranching, military, and commuting families and is dominated by Belt Public Schools, a K–12 school with a total enrollment of 300 students, 95 of whom are in high school.

Through his work to establish a monthly public prose and poetry reading, which he cannily named 'Belt it Out,' at The Belt Theater (c. 1916), a local historical landmark that seems to be perpetually under restoration, Ross learned a great deal about cowboy poetry, his personal muse, and becoming a teacher in a rural place.

Chapter 9: Bridging Divides Through Place-Based Research, or What I Didn't Know About Hunting in the Northern Rockies

Hali Kirby-Ertel shares her experiences as an English teacher in a K-12 school of about 230 students in Gardiner, Montana, a town of 800 permanent residents along the north entrance to Yellowstone National Park. As a new teacher, Kirby assigned an argumentative paper on hunting without realizing the deep divide in the community between ranching families and the naturalists and biologists working in the Park. Her story of refining her pedagogical goals to meet the unique needs of the Gardiner community offers insight into the process of overcoming the 'stranger teacher' identity and the role of a talented teacher designing specific curricula to bring the community together.

Chapter 10: Whose Kids Are They, Anyway? Balancing Personal and Professional Identities in a Rural School

Kari Patterson had always planned to marry a rancher and live in the foothills of the Bridger Mountains, so, when she graduated from college in Montana 30 years ago, she immediately began seeking a rural teaching position there. She shares stories of her job search, which included applying for an English teacher/wrestling coach position before landing a job teaching English, reading, science, art, home economics, physical education, health, and even cheerleading. Patterson describes how she grew from a young teacher who, in her zeal to be everything she felt a teacher of all these subjects had to be, became overly immersed in her students' lives, to a professional educator contentedly watching seniors graduate every year. Throughout she highlights her unique experiences of teaching in a rural community.

Chapter 11: Teaching and Learning at Nay Ah Shing School

Together, Gregg Rutter, a K-12 Gifted and Talented Education Coordinator; Roger Nieboer, a Reading Coordinator: Govinda Budrow, a fourth grade teacher: and Bambi O'Hern, a fifth grade teacher, represent a diversity of background experience and time at Nay Ah Shing School, a tribal community school serving families of the Mille Lacs Band on the Ojibwe reservation in Minnesota. They share stories of working with students and setting school and student learning goals. Additionally, they discuss conceptions and misconceptions of deficits in their community and school, conceptions of gifted and talented learners, and teacher challenges and opportunities in the school and community. They also reflect on how, as teachers at Nay Ah Shing, they have changed and grown over time.

Chapter 12: Teaching in My Own Voice: A 30-Year Pedagogical Journey

Sharon Bishop reflects on her 30-year career teaching English Language Arts at a rural school in Nebraska in this chapter. When she started teaching in 1979, she was just as bewildered by the community as many of the early teachers who shared their stories in the first section of this book; she traces her development as a teacher through years of consolidation, infusion of technology, and the pendulum swing of educational policy. She credits the 'latitude' she was given to develop curricula as a primary factor in her long and productive career and describes the development of her unique teaching identity and voice.

We invite you to move forward to Part I and enter into the narrative worlds of our rural literacy teachers. Whether you are a rural, suburban, or urban educator, a pre-service teacher or a teacher with 30 years of experience, we believe the stories in this volume will enrich your understanding of, and appreciation for, rural youth in rural spaces and the teachers who love them.

Acknowledgements

We thank the early reviewers of this book proposal for their time and thoughtful suggestions. We also thank Routledge publisher Naomi Silverman for her support of our work and her recognition of the importance of the issues we address.

We also thank the book's contributors and their rural students, who taught us much about literacy teaching and learning in rural schools.

References

Bal, M. (1999). *Introduction to the theory of narrative* (2nd ed.). Toronto: University of Toronto Press.

Booth, W. C. (1961). *The rhetoric of fiction*. Chicago, IL: University of Chicago Press.

Bruner, J. (1986). *Actual minds, possible worlds*. Cambridge, MA: Harvard University Press.

Campbell, J. (1972). *Myths to live by*. New York, NY: Viking.

Connelly, F. M., & Clandinin, D. J. (2006). Narrative inquiry. In J. Green, G. Camilli, & P. Elmore (Eds.), *Handbook of complementary methods in education research* (3rd ed.) (pp. 477–487). Mahwah, NJ: Lawrence Erlbaum.

Donehower, K., Hogg, C., & Schell, E.E. (2007). *Rural literacies*. Carbondale, IL: Southern Illinois University Press.

Frye, N. (1964). *The educated imagination*. Bloomington, IN: Indiana University Press.

Green, B., & Corbett, M. (2013). *Rethinking rural literacies: Transnational perspectives*. New York, NY: Palgrave Macmillan.

Jahn, M. (1999). "Speak, friend, and enter": Garden paths, artificial intelligence, and cognitive narratology. In D. Herman (Ed.), *Narratologies: New perspectives on narrative analysis* (pp. 167–194). Columbus, OH: Ohio State University Press.

Moll, L. C., & Gonzalez, N. (1994). Lessons from research with language-minority children. *Journal of Reading Behavior*, 26(4), 439–456.

Schaafsma, D., Pagnucci, G. S., Wallace, R. M., & Stock, P. L. (2007). Composing storied ground: Four generations of narrative inquiry. *English Education*, 39(4), 282–305.

Theobald, P., and Wood, K. (2010). Learning to be rural: Identity lessons from history, schooling, and the US Corporate Media. In K. A. Schafft & A. Youngblood Jackson, (Eds.) *Rural education for the twenty-first century: Identity, place, and community in a globalizing world* (pp. 17–33). University Park, PA: Pennsylvania State University Press.

1

LITERACY TEACHING AND LEARNING IN RURAL COMMUNITIES

Problematizing Stereotypes, Challenging Myths

Lisa Schade Eckert and Janet Alsup

The dominant narratives describing rural life are those of retreat from or repose in the rural, either nostalgia for a lost, peaceful existence or disdain of an archaic impoverished lifestyle. As cultural narratives often do, these discourses construct realities for rural life—creating a new norm. In contrast, the existing narrative of rural education is one of lack, one of retreat, or one of escape, of teaching students to desire an (equally flawed) urban narrative and recognize the rural as impoverished. As rural educators who have also lived and taught in suburbia, we see how rural education is often understood through normalizing deficit metaphors—what isn't 'normal' and present, as opposed to what is—and we are particularly saddened by how these understandings affect the teachers and young people in rural spaces. This is particularly important as "growth in rural school enrollment continues to outpace non-rural enrollment growth in the United States, and rural schools continue to grow more complex with increasing rates of poverty, diversity, and students with special needs" (Johnson, Schowalter, Klein, and Lester, 2014, p. 28).

The goal of this book is to problematize these dominant narratives, examine their ideological and cultural foundation and interrupt them through authentic, alternative narrative rural voices. We seek to explore these narratives as they relate to education and schooling and examine the less-recognized, indeed, often ignored or unheard, narratives of secondary school literacy teachers who have experience in rural schools. We hope to contest the constructed reality of rural as framed by educational policy which assesses schools based on test scores and percentage of free and reduced lunch, and to examine ways in which we, as teacher educators, may be complicit in perpetuating this narrative even if it's simply by neglecting to offer an alternative concept of rural as diverse and unique, a teaching position that can offer significant opportunities for pedagogical and personal growth. We do not seek to essentialize rural people/places but to provide a cross-cultural consciousness that recognizes and problematizes dominant conceptions of diversity, and of how teachers and students learn about and from each other in a symbiotic relationship that isn't culture-blind, but also isn't biased. We engage in theorizing the experiences of rural teachers to seek a delicate balance: seeing the uniqueness in the different cultural realities of 'rural' while not exoticizing it as a conception of 'other.' As Reid et al. (2010) write, "Coming to know a place means recognizing and valuing the forms of social and symbolic capital that exist there, rather than elsewhere" (p. 272). The stories in this collection often narrate such illuminating coming to know.

Through the narratives in this collection, we explore ways in which English education programs can help teacher candidates and practicing teachers better understand rural contexts and make informed pedagogical and personal life choices to alleviate potential identity clashes. We believe that teaching and learning involves so much more than quantitative, summative data assessments and hope to bring attention to other ways of thinking about rural schooling to ultimately develop a richer, fuller narrative understanding and appreciation for the unique, challenging, yet fulfilling and often joyous nature of teaching in rural communities. Similar to Reid et al. (2010), we are concerned with "how these relationships constitute rural social space in ways that can be understood (and demystified) by teacher educators, employers and communities, for teachers and students moving into it for the first time" (p. 269). In so doing, we explore larger issues that inform teacher preparation programs and those working with early career teachers developing personal pedagogies. When a significant population in national education is silenced and marginalized, celebrating their voices becomes an issue of social justice to everyone.

Defining 'Rural': Epistemological and Ontological Considerations

Defining 'rural' is not a straightforward task; any homogenous signifier such as 'rural' and 'urban' sets up a false dichotomy of otherness, categorizing and diminishing communities and essentializing the breadth of experiences and ways of living that flourish in unique settings. We believe it is necessary to go beyond essentialist quantitative factors, such as those established by the US Department of Education (see Table 1.1), to broaden those parameters in order to consider the varied size and shape of communities that constitute rural/urban identity, and to be inclusive of cultural, sociological, economic, and geographical factors. We argue that rurality and urbanity, as concepts, are simultaneously epistemological (defined and knowable) and ontological (a way of being).

We both come from families in rural, farm communities, Janet in Missouri and Lisa in Illinois. We then went on to teach in rural schools as well. Lisa's experience with schools that meet the federal definition of 'rural' spans disparate communities: from an elite, affluent resort town in the northern rocky mountains

TABLE 1.1 Department of Education

Fringe	Census-defined rural territory that is less than or equal to 5 miles from an urbanized area, as well as rural territory that is less than or equal to 2.5 miles from an urban cluster
Distant	Census-defined rural territory that is more than 5 miles but less than or equal to 25 miles from an urbanized area, as well as rural territory that is more than 2.5 miles but less than or equal to 10 miles from an urban cluster
Remote	Census-defined rural territory that is more than 25 miles from an urbanized area and is also more than 10 miles from an urban cluster

struggling with remote access via one circuitous, and dangerous, mountain road, to an impoverished but proud tribal community school off the shores of Lake Superior struggling to meet state requirements or face across-the-board firing of indigenous faculty and administration. The context of teaching and learning in each of these communities is very different, each with its own pedagogical challenges; the only constant is the need for knowledgeable, talented teachers to respond appropriately to each context. Janet's experience with rural schooling is likewise varied. She began teaching in a very small (300 students K-12), working-class school in central Missouri that only had textbooks and facilities as a result of property taxes from a local nuclear plant, and she now teaches in a large university town surrounded by many small, yet proud, rural communities in the state of Indiana, which, incidentally, is currently seeking to add "hunting, fishing and the commercial production of meat" as unalienable constitutional rights. Despite the professional journeys we have taken over the years, we both continue to see ourselves to a certain extent as rural people, as rural teachers, at heart.

Rural communities exist in every state in the US, and though 'official' definitions of rural also exist, as we've discussed above, we have, through our interaction with rural teachers from many states, also come to understand that 'rural' as an identity marker is largely ontological. We agree that "the meanings of rural lives and communities are what make rural education research *rural*—not a geographic boundary, low population density, or remoteness" (Howley, 2009, p. 2). One can live outside of a community that meets the federal definition of rural, yet subscribe to or perform a rural identity. One can live in a rural community and not subscribe to a rural identity. We have found that teachers, parents, and students often self-identify as rural even in schools and communities that do not technically meet the demographic requirements set forth by the federal government. We locate those meanings in the narratives of teachers who have lived them; the lived realities of those who teach and reside in rural communities and participate in a particular rural discourse community.

Meanings and relationships embedded in teacher narratives offer opportunities for analysis; theorizing the struggles for early career teachers and the successes of mid- to late-career teachers who successfully participate in community discourses—why do some teachers flounder in rural schooling environments while other teachers thrive? What is unique about the role of teacher as representative of 'outside' culture and ideas in rural communities? How can we better prepare pre-service teachers for rural schooling environments—or provide them with context enough to make informed decisions about job choice? How do we build the foundation of identity development strategies that will better enable teachers to envision the realities of teaching in rural areas? The intersections of personal, community, and professional spaces are particularly relevant in rural communities—as the teacher is often embedded in various groups within the larger society. We know these questions are relevant to all teachers, not just those who are considering a job in a rural district, but we also know that these are most often contextualized with research, examples, and data from urban and suburban centers in most texts and lectures. Again, the rural is omitted.

Rurality, Suburban Normativity, and Urban Research

Public educational policy establishes suburban middle-class white education as normative, resulting in a deficit approach to education; this complicates matters for rural and urban schools which must conform to the standards that operate within an ideological and cultural norm that might have little relation to their community norms and discourses. Recognition of community-specific funds of knowledge (see Hogg, 2011, for review of research defining and extending funds of knowledge) and a wider definition of literacies is diminished, if not completely dismantled, as a result of normative educational policy. Those cultural contexts, including dialect, race, socioeconomic status, and student exceptionalities, which officially constitute diversity, are often conceptualized and defined based on urban demographics by politically motivated national standards; as a result, research and curricular materials supporting culturally responsive pedagogies often come from urban centers. Culturally responsive teaching includes understanding of the culture specific to an individual's teaching context (Gere and Berebitsky, 2009, p. 253), yet little research addresses rurality itself as a reflection of diverse cultural contexts. Even though many rural schools may seem homogenous, they likely serve a student population coming from diverse backgrounds such as farming, ranching, living on Indian reservations or in tribal communities, living in Hutterite or Amish communities, migrant workers, the retired affluent, or even low-wage laborers who are all, regardless of race or socioeconomic status, often marginalized when compared to more affluent 'town' (i.e., suburban) students. More to the point, emphasizing rural communities as culturally diverse in terms of wealth or parental/familial occupation doesn't 'count' as being culturally responsive.

Because national policy constructs the national educational story most addressed in the public sphere, which consists of seemingly endless discourse surrounding the 'fixing' of education, this story becomes the norm that frames statistic-driven discourse that is perceived as inclusive of all schooling. For example, there is much media talk, often reflected in policy maker's discourse, about the failure of inner city schools and the politicized efforts to save these schools through national educational reform (see Menifield, Rose, Homa, and Brewer Cunningham, 2001; Theobald and Wood, 2010, for an analysis of such media discourse and national education policy). While it is true that *some* urban schools deal with severe challenges to their educational missions, including widespread poverty, difficulty speaking English, school mobility, classroom discipline, and certain health and safety risks (see US Department of Education, 2006), the result is often the widespread belief that all school problems and needs are in the urban centers and, conversely, that all urban centers are rife with pervasive school problems. The concept of urbanity, therefore, is equally essentialized and classified as the concept of rurality. Suburban, conversely, is the norm—privileged and without need—representing the vision of high achieving public schools to which both rural and urban should aspire. Thus, by creating a vision of schooling that is far removed from the realities of urban and rural areas, the normative standardization marginalizes communities, schools, students, and teachers who live and work in them. Note, too, the media hype surrounding the film *Waiting for Superman*, which focuses on New York City public and charter schools, a far cry from the public and charter schools located in Hannahville, a small town in the Upper Peninsula of Michigan—yet the film's narrative became the frame for education and policy discussion in communities like Hannahville and those of all shapes and sizes across the country. This drives discourse in ways that are as far removed from rural education as using the New York City subway system as a frame for discussing what public transportation between Gillette, WY, and Glasgow, MT, should look like. More to the point is that while there are certainly similarities among students and schools in all US geographic areas, there are also place-specific successes and challenges. While there is no singular or unitary rural, urban, or suburban student (or teacher) identity, it must be recognized that place does make a difference to students and teachers. As White and Reid (2008) write about teacher education and rural schools, "Focused attention to the relationships in and between places can better prepare pre-service teachers in rural and metropolitan teacher education settings to enter and work in places that are different from their own" (pp. 8–9).

Literacy Teachers as Organic and Public Intellectuals

The role of the public intellectual is applicable to all teachers because educators have the capacity to enact curricula and participate in public discourses that build trust and community (Selvester and Summers, 2012). Literacy teachers in rural communities have a unique capacity, even responsibility, as leaders in arts and humanities in the school which serves as a central meeting space, to enrich the intellectual and creative activities of the community without overstepping boundaries and by recognizing the cultural values and funds of knowledge already present. This professional role may be especially problematic for new teachers who are already dealing with the shock of professional identity development and integrating multiple, sometimes conflicting subjectivities (i.e., teacher/student, authority/friend, child/adult). Add to that the contradictory nature of bridging or translating normative educational policy into the home discourse of a rural community, and the discontinuities can become too much and lead a young teacher to leave the profession. When the teacher embodies educational policy out of touch and out of reach of the unique nature of the community, policy that relies on a standardized label for achievement and success, it becomes more difficult for him or her to connect with the community. In summary, defining and attempting to ensure quality teaching and learning across the board based on normative models sets up new teachers to fail to assimilate into the community—teachers can't design instructional methods tailored to their students and communities because they aren't allowed the freedom to do so.

For example, one may only think of the recently created Common Core State Standards, which have been adopted by 43 states, to see an example of increased standardization, regardless of community identities. For new teachers, this standardization exacerbates fears and already contested aspects of self, which may make it even more difficult to stay in the rural school; a teacher may feel overwhelmed and seek a school or community environment where there may be less of a clash between personal and professional identities, particularly if a teacher is not from a rural community and has little experience living in one. Developing a teaching identity can be an inherent contradiction in any situation; teaching in a rural school can make it even more so.

How do teachers cope with new accountability yet respond to the needs of students and community? How do they navigate the contradictory tendencies exacerbated in rural schools where teachers are often negotiating personal and pedagogical identities in a community which also requires identity change and negotiation for them personally? As teacher educators we even wonder if our own programs serve to convince teacher candidates, even those from rural communities, that teaching in an urban or suburban community is better, more respected, and more worthwhile. Is it possible that we deprogram the rural identity out of all pre-service teachers through our suburban, urban discourse with its assumed link to cultural capital, and only then have to reprogram them when they take jobs in rural communities? Perhaps this programming begins much earlier than in college even, as students as early as the kindergarten years begin to understand, through media, political, and educational discourse, that rural equals deficient.

Socially Just Preparation for All Teaching Environments, Even Rural

As we stated earlier, we're writing this book out of concern about the lack of information regarding all of the above as part of pre-service or in-service teachers' repertoire, even though, should they decide to accept a teaching position in a rural community, developing curriculum becomes the central concern for rural teachers. As we indicated previously, we offer these narratives to contest the narratives of lack that permeate general ideology and discussion of rural education and hope to provide teachers with a depth of knowledge about teaching in rural communities that better prepares them to effectively navigate the pedagogical landscape of schools and communities of any size. Knowing more about teaching in rural environments as well as suburban and urban is imperative for *any* teacher, as we also hope to encourage all teachers to become active in national teaching organizations like the National Council of Teachers of English (NCTE), the International Reading Association (IRA), and their state/regional level affiliates like the Michigan Council of Teachers of English (MCTE), the Missouri Association of Teachers of English (MATE), the Indiana Teachers of Writing (ITW), and the Montana Association of Teachers of English Language Arts (MATELA). We are encouraged by scholarship that demonstrates how practicum experiences in rural contexts help to shift pre-service teachers' conceptions of rurality in general, and rural schools, teachers, and students more specifically. For example, Todd and Agnello (2006), in their study of pre-service teachers and rural teaching, explain how, even though the pre-service teachers they studied initially "perceived that the rural school would be inferior to urban/suburban schools" (p. 180), close interaction with rural teachers dispelled this notion and, as a result, students were better prepared to work in these environments.

In addition to exploring rural teacher identity, we are interested in exploring the intersections between secondary teacher preparation and rural teaching contexts (Coladarci, 2007). Because of the distance between rural schools and the university (university towns are often separated geographically from rural communities), providing a traditional field experience in a rural setting for students who are concurrently enrolled in a full semester of on-campus coursework is often simply not feasible. Typically, students must remain within short driving distance of campus for the semester during their practicum. Little research has focused specifically on exploring alternative models for providing field experiences in rural communities in the United States. Current scholarship explores online teaching methods designed to prepare teachers to teach in online programs aimed at rural students as opposed to actually living and working in a rural community (Compton, Davis, and Mackey, 2009; Hannum, Irvin, Banks, and Farmer, 2009), connecting graduate students who are already living in rural communities to the university campus (Jung, Galyon-Keramidas, Collins, and Ludlow, 2006), or investing in equipment requiring specialized personnel rather than bringing the college students to rural classrooms. While these initiatives and programs are certainly interesting and have great promise, the narratives in this book may enlighten and inform teacher educators and teacher education students in traditional teacher education programs and methods classes who are still perhaps learning about teaching in rural places from a distance. As identity can "involve the construction and reconstruction of meaning through stories over time" (Rodgers and Scott, 2008, p. 733), we hope that the stories told and contextualized by the teachers in this volume will provide useful and transformative narrative experience and understanding for those teachers and teacher candidates reading them.

Teacher Identity and Rural Teacher Identity

As an important part of this book is about the development and sustenance of the rural teacher identity, it only seems fitting that we provide a brief overview of notable scholarship on teacher identity development and how it relates to the rural educator. In the last decade there has been an increase in scholarly interest in teacher identity development and research studies exploring how teacher identities are navigated and constructed (see Akkerman and Meijer 2011; Alsup, 2006; Beauchamp and Thomas, 2009; Beijarrd, Meijer, and Verloop, 2004; and Niessen, 2007). In these studies the complexity and multiplicity of building a teacher identity are explored, with the majority conclusion that being and becoming a teacher involves the intersection and negotiation of multiple, discontinuous, and often contradictory identity positions that together construct a useful and consistent sense of teacher self often through dialogical experience. In other words, in any geographic setting, becoming and being a teacher is a complex task, comprised of the intersection, and contextual selection, of many different senses of 'I,' e.g., student, authority, parent, husband, wife, partner. Enacting the teacher identity involves a negotiation, sometimes even interior dialogue between (Akkerman and Meijer, 2011) these multiple subjectivities resulting in classroom decision making that is hopefully appropriate, honest, and effective.

We assert that while these same sort of research-based understandings of teacher identity development certainly apply to the rural educator, the act of being and becoming a rural teacher is also qualitatively different than becoming a teacher in another place-based setting (e.g., suburban, urban), particularly for the majority of pre-service educators graduating from mainstream colleges of education. The goal of this book is to explicate and interrogate these differences through the narratives of real rural teachers while contextualizing these experiences through current scholarship in rurality, place-based education, teacher identity, and teacher education.

References

Akkerman, S. F., & Meijer, P. C. (2011). A dialogical approach to conceptualizing teacher identity. *Teaching and Teacher Education*, 27(2), 308–319.

Alsup, J. (2006). *Teacher identity discourses: Negotiating personal and professional spaces*. Mahwah, NJ: LEA/NCTE.

Beauchamp, C., & Thomas, L. (2009). Understanding teacher identity: An overview of issues in the literature and implications for teacher education. *Cambridge Journal of Education*, 39(2), 175–189.

Beijaard, D., Meijer, P. C., & Verloop, N. (2004). Reconsidering research on teachers' professional identity. *Teacher and Teacher Education*, 20, 107–128.

Coladarci, T. (2007). Improving the yield of rural education research: An editor's swan song. *Journal of Research in Rural Education*, 22(3). Retrieved May 23, 2008, from http://jrre. psu.edu/22–3.pdf.

Compton, L., Davis, N., & Mackey, J. (2009). Field experience in virtual schooling: To be there virtually. *Journal of Technology and Teacher Education*, 17(4), 459–477.

Gere, A. R., & Berebitsky, D. (2009). Standpoints: Perspectives on highly qualified English teachers. *Research in the Teaching of English*, 43(3), 247–262.

Hannum, W.H., Irvin, M.J., Banks, J.B., & Farmer, T.W. (2009). Distance education use in rural schools. *Journal of Research in Rural Education*, 24(3). Retrieved June 5, 2011, from http://jrre.psu.edu/articles/24–3.pdf.

Hogg, L. (2011). Fund of knowledge: An investigation of coherence within the literature. *Teaching and Teacher Education*, 27, 666–677.

Howley, C. (2009). Critique and fiction: Doing science right in rural education research. *Journal of Research in Rural Education*, 24(15). Retrieved August 10, 2011, from http://jrre.psu.edu/articles/24–15.pdf.

Johnson, J., Schowalter, D., Klein, R., & Lester, C. (2014). *Why rural matters: The condition of rural education in the 50 states.* Washington, DC: The Rural School and Community Trust.

Jung, L.A., Galyon-Keramidas, C., Collins, B. & Ludlow, B. (2006). Distance education strategies to support practica in rural settings. *Rural Special Education Quarterly*, 25(2), 18–24. Retrieved May 29, 2011, from http://search.ebscohost.com/login.aspx?direct=true&db=a9h&AN=21639966.

Menifield, C. E., Rose, W. H., Homa, J., & Brewer Cunningham, A. (2001). The media's portrayal of urban and rural school violence: A preliminary analysis. *Deviant Behavior: An International Journal*, 22, 447–464.

Niessen, T. (2007). *Emerging epistemologies. Making sense of teaching practice.* Maastricht University: Unpublished Doctoral Dissertation. Available online at http://arno.unimaas.nl/show.chi?fid=11066.

Reid, J., Green, B., Cooper, M., Hastings, W., Lock, G., & White, S. (2010). Regenerative rural social space? Teacher education for rural-regional sustainability. *Australian Journal of Education*, 54(3), 262–276.

Rodgers C.R., & Scott, K.H. (2008). The development of the personal self and professional identity in learning to teach. In M. Cochran-Smith, S. Feiman-Nemser, D. J. McIntyre, & K.E. Demers (Eds.), *Handbook of research on teacher education: Enduring questions in changing contexts* (3rd ed., pp. 732–755). New York, NY: Routledge.

Selvester, P. M., & Summers, D.G. (2012). *Socially responsible literacy: Teaching adolescents for purpose and power.* New York, NY: Teachers College Press.

Theobald, P., & Wood, K. (2010). Learning to be rural: Identity lessons from history, schooling, and the US Corporate Media. In K. A. Schafft & A. Youngblood Jackson (Eds.), *Rural education for the twenty-first century: Identity, place, and community in a globalizing world* (pp. 17–33). University Park, PA: Pennsylvania State University Press.

Todd, R. H., & Agnello, M. F. (2006). Looking at rural communities in teacher preparation: Insight into a P-12 schoolhouse. *Social Studies*, 97(4), 178–184.

US Department of Education. (2006). NCES urban-centric locale categories. *Rural education in America*. Retrieved April 5, 2013, from http://nces.ed.gov/surveys/ruraled/page2.asp.

White, S., & Reid, J. (2008). Placing teachers? Rural schooling through place-consciousness in teacher education. *Journal of Research in Rural Education*, 23(7), 1–11. Retrieved September 1, 2011, from http://jrre.psu.edu/articles/23-7.pdf.

PART I

From Stranger to Native: Early Career Teacher Narratives

2

FROM STRANGER TO NATIVE: EARLY CAREER TEACHER NARRATIVES

Lisa Schade Eckert and Janet Alsup

It is a commonplace that new teachers, no matter where they teach, are presented with many personal and professional challenges. Teaching in a rural school is both no different than teaching in any other school, and very different, as the narratives in this section exemplify. Some of the experiences the new teachers narrate could happen to a new teacher in any geographical area, such as shifting understandings of self, students who are difficult to motivate, or the pressures of high stakes testing. Other experiences narrated in these four chapters seem to describe events and situations specific to teaching in a rural setting, such as lack of school funding or subpar facilities, expectations of a tight-knit, multigenerational community, and the expression of ideologies and subjectivities common to rural culture.

Donehower, Hogg, and Schell (2012) define rural geographically, demographically, and culturally (p. 7). As shared in the Introduction, there are government definitions that use demographic and geographic data to describe what is meant by rural in the US. However, and perhaps as interesting to the new teachers in this chapter, is the definition of rural that is more about culture or community. Donehower et al. (2012) write,

> It is important to define rural not only demographically and geographically, but culturally as well. The word *rural* functions for many as a marker of identity, regardless of demographic criteria or current location. People may self-identify as rural or identity others as rural, and by so doing invoke a complex chain of associations and ideologies.
>
> (p. 7)

These cultural markers of rural life and identity are perhaps the most important aspects of rural life and present the most serious challenges for the young teachers in the following chapters—even those who grew up in rural areas or small towns themselves.

Taylor, Jeff, Kendra, and Chea all find themselves in unfamiliar territory in the rural school, and this unfamiliarity perhaps exaggerates their feelings of difference or otherness. They have a hard time coming to terms with what they see as the very different ways their students think about education, careers, family, and even recreation. It takes time for them to reject these stereotypes born from feelings of alienation and feel at home in the rural school and community. New teachers in any setting will experience identity shifts from 'student' to 'teacher'; however, such ideological shifts in understanding, more related to community than to professional subjectivity, were real and profound for the teachers in the chapters who marked themselves as children of suburbia.

Emerging Themes in Early Career Narratives

In the narratives that follow, there are several themes, issues, or ideas that emerge as central to the professional lives of the four early career teachers in this book, Taylor, Jeff, Kendra, and Chea. Each of these themes can arguably be understood as specific to rural teaching, at least as it was experienced by the teacher who tells the story. Each of the authors offers an opportunity to reflect upon rural teaching, particular as a young, new English teacher.

Politics and Policies

A theme common in this first section addresses local, state, and even national policies and politics and their effect on the rural school. Chea's and Kendra's chapters are perhaps most interesting here as they speak about standardized testing and the stress of preparing students and dealing with the fallout from colleagues and community when scores are not as high as expected. Chea in particular talks about how, in her second year of teaching at Southern Wells Junior/Senior High School, testing dominated her teaching life; she felt intense pressure to help her students pass the Indiana state exams. She did make headway, but it almost pulled her apart from her students, and from everything she loved about teaching. Kendra had a similar experience, as she worked toward her students' passing both the state and AP exams; they did well in the end, but Kendra moved on anyway to her next adventure—in another rural school. While Kendra did not see the standardized tests interfering with her instruction and connection with students as much as Chea perhaps did, it still influenced her experience as a first-year teacher. While every teacher in any public school in the US may experience such pressures and stressors, Chea and Kendra seemed to feel them more deeply because of their isolation (the only one, or one of few, English teachers in the school) and visibility (the sense of being blamed by the close-knit community for any literacy deficiencies).

Other issues specific to rural schools experienced by the authors in the narratives that follow are long commutes to work, sharing classrooms due to lack of space, old or outdated texts because of rigid approval systems and/or lack of funding, and a small community of colleagues with years of experience and their own habits and ways of doing things. Policies and politics, while they certainly affect all teachers, seem to have a special stronghold in the rural school.

Importance of Teacher Autobiography

It may not be a new idea that the experiences one brings to a new job change how one experiences it. When becoming a teacher, such past experiences may be even more important simply because of the number of years we have all spent in school, the number of years we have observed teachers doing their jobs. Such an "apprenticeship of observation" (Lortie, 1975) can cause new teachers to teach as they remember being taught. Also, in Alsup's (2006) study, the teacher who had the smoothest transition into the profession were the ones who experienced the least tension in this transition, the ones whose professional environments closely matched their own school experiences as a student and who saw little tension between their beliefs and subjectivities and those reflected in the school culture (p. 182). However, when new teachers had to make sense of a school culture or environment very different from their own past experiences, beliefs, or expectations, they experienced tension and only persevered in the profession if they were able to make complex connections between their own perceptions and expectations and the school's identity. The authors of the narratives that follow all describe how they did just that—made connections between themselves and their new school cultures, environments that seemed at first alien to them.

It can be argued that each of the teachers in these chapters engage in what Alsup (2006) calls "borderland discourse," or

> discourse in which disparate personal and professional subjectivities are put into contact toward a point of integration. Such integration can lead to cognitive, emotional, and corporeal changes, resulting in identity growth or increased metacognitive awareness.
>
> (p. 205)

Autobiography or personal experiences are important. They help to create personal ideologies, subjectivities, and beliefs, and they change how we think about our professional and personal lives. The authors here are no exception; they likewise brought their personal histories to their new jobs and they had to negotiate tensions between their internalized understandings of teaching and learning and the new expectations and assumptions reflected in the rural culture around them.

Stereotypes and Cultural Markers

Related to the above theme is the theme of teacher perceptions of stereotypical thinking or behavior in the rural culture. Understandings of the rural are awash with stereotypes in the media, in music, in movies, and within images. One doesn't have to look far to find them, starting with *Duck Dynasty* and *Rocky Mountain Bounty Hunters*, and ending with the Redneck Comedy Tour and country songs about tractors, taverns, and trains. Donehower et al. (2007) describe stereotypes about the literacy of rural people as well (pp. 45–54). They write how rural people have been stereotyped as less intelligent or literate than those from urban or sub-urban areas. This division of 'high' and 'low' cultures can be linked to social class, gender, and racial hierarchies that serve to empower a certain group over another (p. 47); educators may have participated in this ranking of culture (and people) and even perpetuated it, as they are often themselves stereotyped and even scapegoated for not raising all students to a certain level of literacy.

The four new teachers in the following chapters all admit to harboring stereotypes of rural students and culture, including such beliefs as they are unintellectual (or even hostile toward education), love tractors and trucks, plan to be farmers or factory workers, use poor grammar, are often racist and sexist, and come from abusive or poor families. While it may be true that some of the students in the schools do exhibit such behaviors or identities, it seems as if the new teachers sometimes 'othered' their students to the extent that they had difficulty finding any sense of connection to them.

Sherman and Sage (2011) conducted a study in which they explored perceptions of education in a rural town in California after an economic collapse. They found that how education was valued in the community differed according to a family's social and moral standing; children from poor or struggling families were sometimes assumed by schools to be uneducable and therefore destined to remain in often economically depressed rural areas, similar to their parents (pp. 11–12). Sherman and Sage argue that teachers and schools must not perpetuate such social, moral, and class distinctions, but should instead provide equitable encouragement and support for all students (p. 1).

For the teachers in this section, their students might as well have been from a different planet—at first, anyway. As their first years of teaching continued, however, the new teachers found ways to make connections, began to see the students more as complex, interesting human beings rather than cardboard rural cutouts. They began to understand them and their culture not as 'less' but as simply different—a difference that they started to like.

Community and Place

A fourth theme of importance in the chapters that follow is the centrality of community, place, and geography to the culture of the rural school. Each of the authors describes how the students and other teachers/administrators in his or

FOREWORD

Leslie Susan Rush

I must begin this foreword by making an admission: I grew up in the suburbs of Dallas, Texas.

In spite of my suburban beginning, I have been fortunate to live much of my adult life in rural communities. My first classroom teaching position was in rural Uganda, east Africa, where I taught A-level literature, prose, and poetry to high school students whose parents farmed in villages neighboring Lake Albert. I was so young as a teacher there, but my three years at Duhaga Secondary School in Hoima, Uganda, led to me say thereafter that Uganda was where I really 'grew up.' After another three-year stint teaching sophomore English in the outskirts of Los Angeles (definitely not rural!), I returned home to Texas and taught sophomore and senior English in Farmersville, Texas—home of the Fighting Farmers—in northeast Texas for six years. Since 2002, I have been a faculty member at the University of Wyoming, where I have been responsible for pre-service teacher education in English for this predominantly rural state. Students who completed the English Education program at UW have gone on to be English teachers in a variety of settings, in Wyoming and elsewhere, but many of them would identify themselves and their communities as rural.

As a suburban to rural transplant, I am thrilled to see this book, which enriches our understanding of rurality and of teaching in rurality in such a thoughtful and competent way. I am also deeply honored that the editors chose me to introduce their work to the world.

The editors of this volume, Lisa Eckert and Janet Alsup, think about rural education as an issue of social justice. Frequently when the notion of social justice is bandied about, the context in mind is an urban one, with high population density to accompany issues of poverty, racism, crime, and all the rest of the problems that are frequently attached to urban settings. However, there are plenty of problems such as these to be concerned about in rural settings as well—minus the population density—and the prevalence of rurality in the US speaks to the importance of attending to these problems in rural settings. Like Lisa and Janet, however, I would not have anyone imagining that *rural* is synonymous with *deficit*. The narratives in this lovely book clearly picture the ways in which the beauty and community and collaborative nature of rural people can impact literacy and English teaching.

In this work, nine teacher narratives are presented, organized by experience. We hear from Taylor Norman, Jeff Spanke, Kendra McPheeters-Neal, and Chea Parton who write about their experiences as early career teachers in rural settings. Subsequently, we experience rural teaching with Jeffrey B. Ross, Hali Kirby-Ertel, Kari Patterson, Gregg Rutter, Govinda Budrow, Bambi O'Hern, Roger Nieboer, and Sharon Bishop, all of whom are mid- or late-career teachers. The beauty of their writing and the depth of feeling that these writings evince about the personal experiences of rural teachers help to tell the story of rurality in a specific and consequential way for the lucky readers of this book. By way of introduction of these writers, I would like to address the question of what I am taking away from my reading of their stories.

Several of the narratives speak of the importance of responding—as teachers—in a positive way to our own failures. In almost all cases, whether the failure was a betrayal of an individual's expectations or an unconscious setting up of a situation that proved divisive, the teachers in this book recognize their own failures and see them as opportunities for building. They articulate how they have moved past the prejudice that they brought with them—preconceived and negative notions of rural people, rural schools, and rural communities—in order to become part of the community in which they teach. It is this becoming part of the community, beginning with being an observant stranger, perhaps, but ending—for long-term success—with not attempting to overlay our instruction with a desire to civilize or to convert or to prepare students for a different place that speaks strongly to the importance of self-evaluation. These teachers describe the important work of creating and pulling on connections made with rural geography through cowboy poetry, with rural community history and current events, with rural perspectives on hunting, and even with 'tractor lust.'

What becomes clear through the reading of these stories is that the teachers who have successfully managed the transition from urban or suburban to rural are those who have kept their senses of humor intact and who have embraced the flexibility needed to manage teaching in rural communities. The demands on teachers in rural communities are different from those in suburban or urban ones; so, therefore, should be the way in which rural teachers engage with each other and with the rural communities they serve. These teachers tell the stories of their engagement, their flexibility, and their creativity. It is a flexibility that embraces the culture of the community: hunting; differing ideas about time; the curriculum of place; local control, local literature, local language. All of these unique her school were closely linked to others living in the community—sometimes even historically or genealogically. Jeff writes about how his students would see pictures of their parents, aunts, and uncles in old yearbooks; they were part of a multigenerational school community. Adults still living in the area often knew the older teachers and had attended the school themselves—and, therefore, had opinions about how it could best be run. Sometimes students had to outlive or shake off stereotypical labels that they were just like their father, or mother, or uncle, or aunt. They had to work just to be themselves. Jeff talks about what it's like to be a teacher in a rural school when you don't live in the community; the place, the space becomes less real, less palpable somehow, and the teacher likewise becomes less real to the community. Taylor has to realize that perhaps her students aren't anti-intellectual; they just intellectualize in different ways, and for different reasons. Chea, while she is from a rural area herself, still finds herself feeling like an outsider in this rural school, as she can't remember when she was actually like her students, even if she knew she had to be at some point.

All four teachers describe how at the end of their first or second year of rural teaching, they began to respect the place, see it, feel it, hear it. They began to see the students as not quite so alien and themselves as not quite so different. The geographical space that once separated them from each other seemed to shrink in size, at least metaphorically. The acres of farmland no longer represented a seemingly un-crossable intellectual or emotional gap; it was simply a short hike to the other side.

Identity Shift

As noted earlier, identity shift happens for all, or most, new teachers as they move from being students to teachers, and this identity shift in a rural school is both similar to and different from that in any other environment. The identity shift begins in the first few years of teaching, a shift that occurs when young intellectuals and teachers take what they have learned to the adolescents whom they are instructed to teach with the mission to help them grow, develop, and be inspired. When this idealism is challenged, which it almost always is, it is the job of the young teacher to bounce back, to integrate personal and professional expectations and subjectivities, and find that personally meaningful borderland discourse. Each of the four teachers in these stories, Taylor, Jeff, Kendra, and Chea, found this borderland partially through their recognition of the rural, the reality of rural life and rural people, not the stereotype. Ironically, they found their borderland discourse by negotiating their transition to a literally new geographical space. The metaphorical borderland was found amid Indiana's very real cornfields.

So what can new teachers and teacher educators take away from these stories? We hope that new teachers in rural settings will be inspired to think about their own identities and life experiences and consider how they intersect with the place-based culture of the rural environments in which they teach. Such critical reflection may lead early career teachers in rural areas to integrate place-relevant assignments into their ELA curricula and, more importantly, understand rural spaces as complex and many-faceted, not simple or easily labeled.

References

Alsup, J. (2006). *Teacher identity discourses: Negotiating personal and professional spaces.* Mahwah, NJ, and Urbana, IL: Lawrence Erlbaum/NCTE.

Donehower, K., Hogg, C., & Schell, E. E. (Eds.). (2007). *Rural literacies.* Carbondale, IL: Southern Illinois University Press.

Donehower, K., Hogg, C., & Schell, E. E. (Eds.). (2012). *Reclaiming the rural: Essays on literacy, rhetoric, and pedagogy.* Carbondale, IL: Southern Illinois University Press.

Lortie, D. C. (1975). *Schoolteacher: A sociological study.* Chicago, IL: University of Chicago Press.

Sherman, J., & Sage, R. (2011). Sending off all your good treasures: Rural schools, brain-drain, and community survival in the wake of economic collapse. *Journal of Research in Rural Education*, 26(11), 1–14.

3

A RURAL EDUCATION: FROM STRANGER TO STRANGERER

Taylor Norman

MCCUTCHEON HIGH SCHOOL, LAFAYETTE, INDIANA

I struggle with this. I struggle with putting my background in the rural classroom to language, as I am not sure how to explain my experiences without stereotyping a group or generalizing their reactions. I do not want to do that. What I provide in this chapter is not a set of solutions; it is instead *my* experience and *my* perception of a series of events set in the rural. This experience as well as perception is understood through and narrated by my reaction to, reflection on, and action of educating children in the rural.

> What we want and need is education pure and simple, and we shall make surer and faster progress when we devote ourselves to finding out just what education is and what conditions have to be satisfied in order that education may be a reality and not a name or a slogan.
>
> (Dewey, 1938)

I will use this chapter to illustrate my experiences while working in two different sites. Although different, each site carries similar attributes. They are both labeled rural communities, they are both agrarian, and they both have small populations of diverse, marginalized peoples. However, one site is extremely familiar as it is set in my classroom, and the other site is foreign as it is set in another's classroom. On one site I am a teacher—and the other—a researcher. Through the narration of my perception according to a familiar site, a foreign site, and a change in identity, I hope to explicate my struggling stance on the rural.

I reacted, in the beginning, to my rural classroom from my suburban subjectivity. I found no issue with it; I thought it important that I react from the suburban in order to show the rural students the purpose of an education. As each year passed, though, I began to question how I understood the purpose of an education. I began to struggle with the type of student and the type of knowledge that qualified as education with a purpose. This struggle then led me to reflection, as I came to be an observant stranger in my rural classroom.

While watching their movements, listening to their voices, analyzing their needs, and synthesizing my plan of attack, my suburban purpose of an education took a turn toward my rural students' purpose of an education. Through conversations with my students and a close reading of the current curriculum guide for each of my classes, I worked to reintroduce my students to education—or simply, reintroduce them to the invaluable need to be curious. It was not about college acceptance that I forced an education upon my students (as I had experienced); instead, I used the reaction of our difference, and the reflection of our similarity to perform the action of teaching.

It really is a torrid affair, my relationship with the rural. As an educational researcher today, I am struggling with my purpose in the rural classroom. I do not teach there anymore; I am now only an observer. I have no connection beyond research, which creates a relationship with the students that is less human and more mechanic, as they become my data points. My struggle, although mine, is real, and the story of its continual progress is important, not only to me but to others who struggle with something similar.

Familiar

The first site is somewhere familiar. I taught in a rural high school for four years. The school served a large student body, residents within a large district map (some students drove 45 minutes each day to get to school). The student population could generally be described as mostly white, working-class teenagers. I use these experiences to explain my initial interactions with the rural. I was introduced to this community through my student teaching practicum, at the end of which, I retained the twentieth slot in a large English department.

Reaction

Because I am a child of a suburb in northwest Indiana, I am a stranger to the customs and values of a rural community. Having been born and raised somewhere else, different sorts of values were instilled within me. I was urged to go to college, earn an abundant amount of money, and claim a high status in society based on career choice. This was education's purpose according to us, the children of the suburban. The adults in my community, for the most part, had all three. My friends lived in large houses in expensive subdivisions, mothers with college degrees stayed home to take care of the house and the children, and fathers spent much of their time away on business trips. I can remember one of my friend's homes. Her bedroom was the size of our family's living room. Her mother bought us lavish and expensive lunches and supervised our behavior from the upstairs kitchen while we played pool and watched movies on a theater-sized screen in the basement. Her father was never home, and her mother was apathetic toward her daughter and all her visiting girlfriends. The case was similar at most of my friends' homes. The mother was physically there but consciously absent, the father missing in action, and the children reaping the benefits from their parents' money and status.

Although my parents did not fit this exact mold, it was my casted image as a child. My parents became pregnant with my older sister while in high school. Having been banished from their school as well as the community, my parents married and my father took a job as a toolmaker in a small tool and die shop. My mother mothered. She and my father gave birth to three more children by the time they were both 24 years old. Because my parents had also been children in my hometown, they encouraged us to attain the above-mentioned staples. They urged us to do it as young adults because of their struggles while trying to do so after having children. Parenting as young people, they believe, is why they only attained parts of the community's main values.

My three siblings and I have listened to many speeches attributed to the *right way of doing things* and the *wrong way of doing things*. Subsequently, by the age of eight, I was studying hard in school and obsessively worried about grades. I can remember studying my math workbook in second grade and taking notes for our upcoming test. I knew it was imperative that I do well in school in order to make something successful of myself. As well, I got a job on a blueberry farm at the age of ten, as I started to feel the social pressure of name brand clothing. I spent each summer of my middle school career in a rural community, living with my stepsister, working six days a week, 12-hour days for two months straight. I came home with a load of cash and the ability to participate in my friends' social practices. My mother tried to encourage me to relax in both expeditions, but without knowing it, she had asked it of me. Become educated, make a lot of money, become known in what you do—that was my objective—and without hard work and total concentration, these achievements could not be mine.

This situation is mine, it is personal, and it is ingrained. As a rural teacher, I found myself trying to situate students within my suburban frame. Initially, I reacted to the students as a familiar. Based on the size of the school's faculty and student body, I believed I was entering a school much like my own. Consequentially, I assumed the school was instilling the purposes of education just as I was taught as a student. My assumptions became my students' burden. I created lessons based on their deficiencies. I wanted to tell the students what they were missing, what they could have, and impose upon them the values I believed should have been instilled by their community. In a place where college was not a direction, I directed them. In a place where money was not an ultimate drive to success, I drove them. If a student did not want to go to college, I worked to show him or her the necessity in it. If a student did not want to read a historically significant novel, I worked to convince him or her of the worldly knowledge the book would teach.

I assumed all of the students would go to college. I judged them when they did not. I assumed all of my students wanted to learn in order to get into college. I judged them when they did not. This reaction was, at first, all I had. It was a space of judgment and ridicule. It was a space of horror and disgust. *What do you mean they do not want to learn how to write a complete sentence? What do you mean they do not do or turn in homework?* I can remember asking my mentor teacher these questions during my student teaching practicum. Shock does not even describe it—I was angry. No one had ever had this conversation with me. I was upset to be learning it now; I was upset that I had no methodological way out. I did not know what to do next. I did not know how to teach students who did not want to learn. Every year in my undergraduate pre-service teaching program, I had theorized of a classroom full of students who wanted to learn. Learning later that this was not true felt like total betrayal.

For the first two years in my rural community, I maintained the values of my childhood community. I scoffed at the students' inability to do homework, and spent endless hours lecturing them about the importance of completing class work. Nothing changed, though; they did not worry when homework was incomplete. They experienced knowledge without respect or understanding or concern for my named purposes for its consumption. They had future careers in the family business. If the family did not have a business, many of the students took apprenticeships by their senior year to learn a skilled trade and make a career of it. Few students spoke of college as a future option, although, many were incredibly capable.

I began to understand that as my community had instilled higher education as a core value, this community had instilled something else in its place. I realized then that I was approaching my students all wrong. If I wanted them to see the importance or purpose in being educated, I had to stop judging them for their ignorance. Instead, I had to go back to the proverbial drawing board and ask myself, how do I show and not tell my students a (and not the) purpose in education; how do I show them a purpose that is relevant to their (and not my) community?

Reflection

Consequentially, I began to reflect on the effect my strangeness had on the rural classroom. It took me some time and much thought to change my automatic suburban reaction. I contemplated different actions based on the experiences of a teacher who is a stranger to her/his teaching community. By the melding of teacher and student values rather than the melting of student for teacher values, I came to be hyper-conscious of asking questions before accepting (or even worse, assuming) answers. This is not to say that my education taught me to melt my students' values; on the contrary, I believe my education taught me to be inclusive of diversity, and creative when dealing with students of unfamiliar communities. Nevertheless, I was struggling.

As I became aware of my judgments, the students became aware of them, too. I began talking openly about their behaviors I once called strange and now called different—not weird but unfamiliar. The students responded well to this dialogue. They shared suggestions with me that would create a classroom environment focused on a reciprocal learning relationship. I learned from them as they learned from me. Our strangeness taught each of us, teacher and student, a new perspective, a new perception. For me, my perspective changed on planning lessons and classroom activities; for the students, their perspective changed on learning lessons and participating in classroom activities. Unlike me, my students did not want to learn to become some huge success; they wanted to learn only if they felt it applied to their everyday lives.

I planned through and with the students instead of planning according to my assumed or accepted educational values. Through this process, the students began to teach me. They taught me to take action for their sake. I no longer taught content relevant to me, but relevant to them. I was finally addressing my own deficiencies as a teacher. No longer did I turn my back on the problem or speak to it in a language lost in translation. By my third year in the classroom, I took action upon the conflicts my values brought to the rural classroom. While repeating the question—how do I show and not tell my students the benefits of education—I pursued a new direction.

Action

I converted from stranger to observant stranger. I never felt like a community member, but I did somehow begin to feel like a stranger aware of our differences, a stranger who was observant and conscious of what could be learned from our differences. This shift in my methodology became most apparent in my junior-level American literature course. Each year I taught American literature, and each year I was left feeling dissatisfied. I would go into each summer hoping the students would take the content seriously the next year. However, once I became aware of our differences through reflection, I realized my approach was missing relevance. I was talking at my students rather than with them.

The difficulty that American literature presented in my rural community was its unimportance in the students' daily lives. The language is archaic in most of our classroom texts. The authors are all dead. They are reciting stories the students have already heard, particularly in their American history class the hour before my class. It became apparent that something must change—I had to learn to change my approach. From unit to unit, I planned around current issues in the community, issues in the school, and issues among the students. I started watching the shows and movies the students mentioned regularly, listening to the music they enjoyed, and reading the books the suggested to me. Through this, the shift in approach occurred. We looked at the social commentary of today in order to relate it to the social commentary of generations past. We started speaking the same language, and to both of our benefit, we enjoyed learning about each other through classroom content.

Subsequently, I decided to teach Upton Sinclair's *The Jungle* because of its fit in the American literature curriculum, and its plot which addressed aspects of my students' current situations. The choice to teach *The Jungle* was not mine; it was a joint decision. I, alone, might have chosen the book, but it was for the sake of my students that I became aware of its need. I read Sinclair's book the summer before I became an undergraduate. For my high school graduation, my mother gave me a box of books, entitled: 'All the books you should have read in high school.' Taking my mother's suggestion, I brought Sinclair's *The Jungle* into my rural class-room after becoming acquainted with my students and their customs. I believed Sinclair's work would fit in both my rural classroom and the course's curriculum. There was one problem though—my school had not approved Sinclair's text.

Several forms and a proposal to the school board later, the book was added to our curriculum and to the shelves of our book room. The anticipation I felt the day I passed the books out was immense. I had put so much planning into this unit plan, and I hoped the students would at least respond a little bit. The melding of my newfound value for their community and their newfound value for learning created a positive experience for both of us. They began to understand American literature from a new perspective, and I began to understand them from a new one as well. Rather than choosing the classroom content based on what I found relevant, I began to listen to my students. The former can be described as planning lessons backward, from teacher to student; the latter as planning lessons forward, from student to teacher.

Although a text with archaic language and a dead author, *The Jungle* allowed for conversations about current issues of immigration relevant in my students' community. Sinclair's work showed a view of immigration many of my students had not yet considered. The plight of Jurgis and Ona spoke to my students imme-diately, which allowed us critical discussions of local and national immigration as well as our community's and nation's social composition. They began to under-stand that no matter the color of an immigrant's skin, their culture will always sep-arate them from the norm; without assimilating, the immigrants stood no chance of achieving the American dream. Additionally, many of my students were farm-ers, and found much interest in the meat packing plants described in the novel. Students were outraged and disgusted when they read the description of a pig being dressed (butchered) in five minutes. They understood the inhumanity for both the workers and the animals through this description. They began to address the industrial revolution in new terms. Most importantly, they were doing their homework, reading the novel, and actively participating in class. It was the largest amount of student participation I had received thus far.

I learned that day to involve my students in classroom planning. But this type of involvement had little to do with lists of choices or elections based on prefer-ence (what I was trained to do when trying to involve my students in classroom planning); instead I utilized what I knew. I was the professional, after all. I studied my students as I studied my content. I used each as research inquiries. While conversing and interrogating my students, I conversed and interrogated my content. I found that this process allowed my students involvement by proxy, because it was through this simultaneous study that classroom planning became a communal venture, one that incorporated, required, and reciprocated student participation. It was not a solution. It was a formula. The solutions created the struggle; the formula brought the struggle to light.

Foreign

Knowing my personal struggle while working in the rural, I returned to college as a graduate student of education on a condition that I would write about what was shared between the rural and me. During my first year as a graduate student I took a course that required I do an ethnographic study based on societal views on race, class, and/or gender. My experiences in the rural classroom caused me to set the ethnographic study in a rural classroom. I wanted to experience the rural classroom as a stranger again and research areas of the rural classroom I never had a chance to as a classroom teacher. The experiences I occurred and the perceptions I came to acquire (rather than assume) for the rural needed some consideration. I thought that a study grounded in this setting would allow me time and opportunity to understand why my initial feelings of resentment and rage turned to empathy and love.

I chose an unfamiliar site with familiar behaviors to focus my study. Of race, class, and gender, I chose gender, specifically gender practices and sexual diversity, on which to hone in. I wanted to understand how the rural reacted to gender practices or sexual diversity that queer the normal (Bower and Klecka, 2009). Behaviors that do not bow down to heterosexual mores, they do not follow the traditional roles of gender appropriation. Instead, those who may be diverse in terms of gender and sexuality are people who ask for the freedom to experience their body as they see fit and not how society sees fit (Slavin-Williams, 2005). According to Bower and Klecka (2009), it is the teacher who is capable of queering the normal, of asking social participants to rethink behaviors named as normal, and of criticizing the customs that accompany normed social behaviors. They challenge teacher educators to bring hetero-normativity and this idea of queering the normal to their classrooms; they challenge teacher educators to begin this rethinking. In agreement, I found reason and purpose for my particular focus. Inquiring within the rural in connection with queering the normal allowed for a narrative of this process.

I planned to approach the research in the same way I did my classroom practice. As a stranger to their community, I first reacted to their stance on gender practices and sexual diversity based on classroom observations. Second, I reflected on those exchanges in accordance with my experiences as a student and a teacher in order to understand their stance. I then used those reflections to construct a survey, which I administered to give voice to their stance on gender and sexual diversity. Like my classroom practice, I wanted to hear from the students. I wanted to know what defined them as a person of their community. Without my content to depend on, when trying to understand a group different from myself, I used my personal perspective to understand their personal perspective on a facet of social dimension. And, like in my classroom, I hoped to find similarity within this difference. I was sure that I would find students who learned a different social narrative about gender and sexuality; however, I was not sure that I would find any similarities. As I was wrong while a practicing classroom teacher, I was wrong again as a beginning educational researcher.

The community I chose was in the classroom of a former colleague. Ms. Bison and I had taught together for a year. The same year I entered graduate school, she moved teaching communities. She moved from the same large rural community I experienced to a small rural community. Ms. Bison and her eleventh grade students became my sources of information about perceptions of gender in a rural community. I spent several days in her classroom over the course of a semester, taking field notes and participating in discussions with both Ms. Bison and her students. What follows is a summary of my own experiences as a classroom teacher that guided and prompted my inquiry into gender perceptions and the rural.

★★★

My first year as a rural schoolteacher, I taught a queer, transgender student. He was in my senior composition course. One of the requirements for this course was a weekly reflection journal focused on life experience. The students were asked to report and reflect on their lives thus far. This male student told stories of teasing and bullying in his early years of school. He began wearing nail polish and growing his hair long as a child because his mother supported it; however, many of his peers and even a few of his teachers found his behaviors unnerving and even deviant. By his senior year, he reported that most of the school community held him at an arm's length. Even though he did not wear skirts or dresses or a full face of makeup, his accented female appearance was enough to leave him feeling alienated, marginalized, and alone. Although he was a resident of this community, he did not belong to this community. The members' silence toward his appearance had a way of silencing his oddity. As an older child and student, he reported in his weekly reflections that he no longer faced as much noticeable discrimination from his peers and little to none from his teachers for wearing high heels, leaving his hair long and styled, and painting his nails.

I was fascinated by the courage of this student. I was amazed at his ability to look the normal in the face and suggest an alternative. Quite honestly, I respected him. I can remember complimenting his high heels one day. His response—"Why do my teachers always compliment the way I look, but my peers only make fun of me?" I did not know how to answer him; but at the same time, I knew exactly what to say to him. Looking back, I wish I had told him that his peers were intolerant and discriminate. I wish I had complimented him on his immense courage; instead, I remember telling him someday people will be more tolerant. I still struggle with some of the responses I shared with my students without the understanding of what should have or could have been said. But that comes from a new place in this struggle, a place that analyzes and synthesizes research, a space that questions human interaction, a stance of a researcher in addition to a teacher.

By my fourth year as a rural schoolteacher things to do with gender and sexuality changed in some respects. The school had formed a gay-straight alliance. I witnessed more students feeling safe to come out in high school rather than during their first year in college. After a student wore a 'straight alliance' T-shirt to school, I read the article another student wrote about the injustice and intolerance this small act perpetuated. And then I taught another queer, transgender student. This student was different from the one I experienced my first year. He was not going to be tolerated; he was going to be acknowledged. He was in my classroom his entire sophomore year.

Through the year, I watched him grow comfortable with his female self. Each day he would come to school clothed in a gradation of the traditional female dress. Some days his face would be in full makeup, some days it would not. Some days he would pair the makeup with a blouse, some days he would accent the two with a barrette in his hair. It was clear, though, that each day he felt more courageous than the day before to be herself. By the end of the school year, he was in full female garb. He turned in assignments with his female name at the top. He seemed happy. I asked him one day how the students treated him and he said to me, "Girl, I don't let those fools get me down." It was the first time he called me "girl," and in that statement, I could feel his strength. Again, I wish I'd told him.

I have had the pleasure of seeing and speaking with each student years after their graduation date. Both are living as women, both are happy, and both stayed in their rural community. One works in salon as an aesthetician and the other works in a restaurant as a server. Both report that they have found their own communities within their rural surroundings.

★★★

These questions of response are why I went back to the rural. I wanted to understand what had changed, if anything, in the community for the transgender students to feel comfortable enough to stay in a town that is generally labeled as bigoted. I chose the focus of gender for the course project in order to see how this specific community and this specific teacher responded to those students who queer the norm. I settled on this direction after attending a lecture on the subject of gender diversity and schools. The speaker spoke about students of the current generation and their open acceptance of diversity, specifically gender and sexual difference. The lecture was based on character definitions of the generation and the media's influence on their social understanding of gender and sexuality in society. The speaker resolved that students of the current generation are more tolerant of gender and sexual difference.

Because my experiences with students and gender diversity aligned with the speaker's, I wanted to ask similar questions in a new but familiar environment. The project then became an inquiry of gender and sexual difference in a rural classroom. My research questions became: To what extent does the observed group of rural students portray the qualities of their defined generation? Next, how do students in the observed rural community react to gender diversity? Finally, how is the rural community's reaction to gender expression different from that of former generations?

Reaction

Initially, I reacted to the students as a researcher and not a teacher. Aware that they belonged to a community of which I am not a member, I sat silently in the back of Ms. Bison's room respecting their space and observing their behaviors. I knew because I did not teach them, that they had no reason to trust me or acknowledge my presence. When they found out I was a good friend of Ms. Bison's, they tepidly began approaching me.

After several classroom visits, I advanced from stranger to semi-stranger. The students began coming up to me regularly. We spent time talking between class and during class. They started asking my opinion on classroom content, as a sort of second opinion to Ms. Bison's. The students were similar to my students. They experienced knowledge without respect or understanding of its purpose. They had future careers in the family business. If the family did not have a business, many of the students took apprenticeships by their senior year to learn a skilled trade and make a career of it. Like my students, regardless of academic skill, few of Ms. Bison's students spoke of college as an option for their future.

This transition from stranger to semi-stranger allowed me to take notice of their enactment of the common character traits of their generation. Based on my initial observations, the students were less tolerant of gender diversity than their more generally defined generation. There was one girl out of all five classes who identified herself as queer, and used any opportunity to discuss it in the classroom. She believed it was important; she thought if her fellow students were confronted with the issue they would become more tolerant. But it was obvious by their eye-rolls and sighs that her statements were falling on deaf ears. I could only imagine their reaction to a boy walking into class wearing four-inch stiletto heels.

Reflection

Reflecting first on classroom interaction between students and Ms. Bison, I witnessed traditional gender practices being both ratified and appropriated during the discussion of their classroom content. While sharing a novel with her class, Ms. Bison read a scene describing a female character undressing. The male students began chanting, and the girl students become red with embarrassment. Interestingly enough, the description of the character undressing encompasses two lines in the novel. The character is told to go change her clothes behind a bus, and one of the male characters "takes notice." The males chanting and the females shying away suggested normalized gendered responses to sex and sexuality. But the strength and quickness of the reaction was what I took notice of—why did they react so fervently to such a small mention of sexuality?

Second, I began to reflect on the one-on-one moments I had with the students and the conversations I overheard them having during unstructured moments in the classroom. Regularly, terms such as 'faggot' and 'gay' were tossed around without acknowledgement of their slander. I was commonly asked if I was married. When I answered no, they asked how old I was. When I stated 29, they suggested I get married soon (alluding to my old age). When I told them I never planned to marry, they looked at me strangely and more times than not told me I was weird or told Ms. Bison her friend was weird. This question and response came from both male and female students, but the female students followed up the last question with one last moment of inquiry. They wanted to know how I was going to have children if I did not get married. I told them that I did not plan to have children, and this created major contortions in their facial expressions.

I was not a stranger to this behavior, though. My students reacted the same way each year I taught in my rural classroom. Regardless of their tolerance toward differences in gender and sexuality, these questions always made me aware of the traditional gender roles at work in my rural community. I could feel through their eyes a similar question: Why would a heterosexual woman choose to participate in abnormal gender practices? After all, is it not a social expectation that a female's duty is to marry and mother children?

Action

Because I had heard conversation and witnessed behaviors of normalized gender and sexuality, I started to construct a survey that asked the students of their perspectives on gender and sexual diversity. The survey was in response to my second research question: How do students in the observed rural community react to gender and sexual diversity? Ms. Bison gave me an entire class period to talk to the students about their stance as well as administer the survey. I introduced the survey to the students by explaining to them my experiences with their generation and its disposition toward gender and sexual diversity.

They talked all hour, reacting to and reflecting on my statements. As the class period progressed, the students began dialoguing with each other. Some conversations created conflict, like that of same-sex couples being allowed at their school dances. Female students giggled and shook their head in total disagreement. Rage erupted among the male students. In one class, one male voice rose among the others, stating that he would knock them down and rip their spines out so they could not dance.

On the other hand, some conversations were calmly assessed. While discussing progressive views on homosexuality, the students, both male and female, agreed that homosexuality was a fad within their generation. They did not believe they were more tolerant, but that students in their generation were grasping at anything to be different. I took note of their agreement. Their shared views suggested a strong level of loyalty among community members. It was obvious they were not going to tell me what I wanted to hear; they were going to serve it to me straight. After our conversation, they spent a few minutes completing the survey.

The survey taught me only one more thing. The students in this rural community gave little thought to gender or sexual diversity. They saw gender and sexual diversity through their community's strong emphasis on family. Without a wife, the husband would have no one to cook for him, to clean the house, to mother his children. Without a husband, the wife would have no children, no one to care for, no purpose. Many female students mentioned their fear of not finding a husband, while many male students felt entitled to a wife. Plain and simple, homosexuality or queer values made few appearances in their thought processes. This was their perspective—and I ask now—was it my duty to change or alter their perspective? Who am I to judge? Bower and Klecka (2009) would say that as a teacher I am a judge of my students' perspectives, and (most definitely) it *is* my duty to change and alter their understanding of normed social practice.

In the end, I return to the lecture I attended. While considering the students' understanding or reaction to nontraditional diversity within gender and sexuality, I am forced to examine the behaviors the students displayed that aligned with their defined generation. The students of today are labeled as "Generation Me" or "GenMe" (Twenge, 2006, p. 4), because they are a generation focused on the individual. These students began graduating high school in 2000 and will continue until 2016. They are the children of the 1960 counterculture. Twenge (2006) asserts that the children of GenMe are said to believe all is possible, they are only satisfied by life if their innermost desires are met daily, and they understand the freedom to be who they are as a right rather than a privilege. They have swollen egos, feel entitled to everything, and generally disregard social approval (Twenge, 2006). Subsequently, they are said to be unaffected by racial or sexual diversity—or that was the suggestion of the lecturer. This suggestion is what started me thinking. If I witnessed intolerance in the rural, gender or otherwise, could that mean rural students are dislocated from their generation?

I remember choosing this study in order to tell the story of a rural community's intolerance regarding sexual and gender diversity. Revisiting my field notes from the course project, I am offered another analysis, one that did not agree with my original hypothesis, one that instead revealed my own biases. This is why the study had to incorporate my experiences in the classroom to understand my stance. My reaction, at first, was suburban. I believed Ms. Bison's students had not witnessed enough of the diversity in the world to understand or even believe that there were students their age who reacted or lived differently. Even when I presented them with videos capturing stories of queer teens, the students responded with bewilderment. These reactions first led me to believe they did not belong to their generation because of their intolerance toward diversity, specifically gender diversity. Yet, something did not fit. It felt uncomfortable. These experiences must tell a different story.

★★★

When I began the project in Ms. Bison's classroom, I was happy to work in a rural classroom. I found little in educational research regarding students who looked like mine. I found, quickly, suggestions made by educational researchers regarding students in the urban (Kozol, 1991; Leistyna, 2002; Valenzuela, 1999). Because of the dilapidated conditions of the American urban school systems, urban students came to hold more precedence over students who were not urban. I learned as an undergraduate in a teacher education program that classrooms were diverse and that teachers must adjust to their students' diversities, but I also learned that students who were of a different race than our own would need the most attention. There was little emphasis on the other facets of multiculturalism such as class or gender. Instead, instruction focused on teachers who worked in underprivileged, poor, urban neighborhoods and their understanding of teaching children in the urban.

When I came back to graduate school, I hoped to bring my experiences in the rural to this multicultural rhetoric. I used Ms. Bison's classroom to analyze my experiences in the rural, both as a stranger and a semi-stranger. Because I came in contact with a culture shock once I realized that the students I thought looked familiar where completely foreign to me, I thought it important that we use the work done in the urban to explain this culture shock. Yet it took time in the rural classroom to understand the multifaceted dimensions of diversity within it and to authentically use methods that I would understand later as culturally responsive teaching and culturally relevant pedagogy (Gay, 2010; Ladson-Billings, 1994). In the urban these methods were most needed as white teachers appeared in minority urban communities planning to save brown and black students with an education similar to their white upbringing. Stripping these communities of their cultural practices in order to dress them in cultural practices that matched that of these foreign teachers in the name of future success was not just unjust, it was plain wrong.

By simply responding to the rural as a culturally constructed community, judgment finds little space. Response is free of judgment; it instead replies within a shared dialogue. Judgment is not a dialogue, it is a monologue, one which narrates only one perspective. As I struggle to find meaning in my stance regarding the rural, I am continually met with feelings of anger, disgust, horror, and outrage; but then, feelings of love, compassion, possibility, and kindness make their way to the surface. In other words, I struggle with explaining how angry I was when I met a group of young people who looked like me but did not want to be educated. I struggle with explaining how easy it was to fall in love with them although we differed significantly.

Simply put, students in the rural are willing to learn. But classic or traditional methods will not always work. It is imperative that teachers get involved. They must become a part of the students' lives in some way, they must begin speaking in the students' language before judging them. Only through this connection can stranger teachers come to understand students from communities unlike their own, clear out the mess of presumptions and judgments, and allow themselves to learn from their students as they teach them. Rather than call them bigots, figure out what they are bigoted toward and teach them a new perspective. Rather than suggest that they all do not know how to write a complete sentence, teach them how based on activities that are relevant outside the classroom. Inspire them and be willing to be inspired by them. Stop with all the anger and outrage, and ask the question: How am I, the stranger teacher, telling and not showing my rural students the larger purpose of learning and curiosity? Through this approach, anger and outrage can turn to love and compassion. This showing means learning a new language, a new way to be. The words I acquired, in both my classroom and Ms. Bison's, changed me. They changed the way I saw the world. They changed my perspective.

There is no easy solution here, but there is a formula, a formula that asks teachers to be conscious and aware of students' presumed differences while noticing their actual differences. In retrospect, I understand now that it was risky, learning their language, learning what we shared in common. But through moments of miscommunication also came communication. As I fumbled with learning the language my students spoke, I learned their words, I learned their connotations, and I learned their purpose. And once I began to use these words, my students started to hear me. It was risky, I guess. It was right, I know.

References

Bower, L., & Klecka, C. (2009). (Re)considering normal: Queering social norms for parents and teachers. *Teaching Education*, 20(4), 357–373.

Dewey, J. (1938). *Experience and education*. New York, NY: Collier.

Gay, G. (2010). *Culturally responsive teaching: Theory, research, and practice* (2nd ed.). New York, NY: Teachers College.

Kozol, J. (1991). *Savage inequalities: Children in America's schools*. New York, NY: Harper Collins.

Ladson-Billings, G. (1994). *The dream keepers: Successful teachers of African American children*. San Francisco, CA: Jossey-Bass.

Leistyna, P. (2002). *Defining & designing multiculturalism: One school system's efforts*. New Albany, NY: State University of New York Press.

Slavin-Williams, R.C. (2005). *The new gay teenager*. Cambridge, MA: Harvard University Press.

Twenge, J. M. (2006). *Generation me: Why today's young Americans are more confident, assertive, entitled—and more miserable than ever before*. New York, NY: Free Press.

Valenzuela, A. (1999). *Subtractive schooling: U.S.-Mexican youth and the politics of caring*. New Albany, NY: State University of New York Press.

4

CROSSING THE TRACKS, OR THE BACON OF DESPAIR

The Story of One Teacher's Story . . . of One Teacher's Story . . . of Teaching in a Rural School

Jeff Spanke

NORTH MONTGOMERY HIGH SCHOOL, CRAWFORDSVILLE, INDIANA

> Son of a son of a son of a farmer.
> I've watched the clock come to dominate my life
> and each morning, like Jonah, I climb into the whale.
> Its power transforms me for better or worse.
>
> —Scott Mutter, *Surrational Images*

> It happens that the stage sets collapse. Rising, streetcar, four hours in the office or the factory, meal, streetcar, four hours of work, meal, sleep, and Monday Tuesday Wednesday Thursday Friday and Saturday according to the same rhythm—this path is easily followed most of the time. But one day the 'why' arises and everything begins in that weariness tinged with amazement. 'Begins'—this is important. Weariness comes at the end of the acts of a mechanical life, but at the same time it inaugurates the impulse of consciousness.
>
> —Albert Camus, *The Myth of Sisyphus*

Overture: Before We Begin

Allow me to set the stage. When I began teaching at a rural Indiana high school in 2008, my first position was the In-School Suspension monitor. As the year progressed, I grew frustrated with the stark contrast between what I expected to find in this new environment and what I actually encountered among students whose backgrounds differed in every conceivable way from mine. For reasons we'll explore below, I took it upon myself to begin writing a novel which chronicled a week in the life of the fictitious Scott Benis: a young, idealistic teacher exiled to a small rural farming community where he too facilitated the ISS room. Though not necessarily autobiographical, the book dawned from my personal anxieties and ultimate depression regarding my status as a 'teacher who doesn't teach.' When I completed the manuscript, I read it once and then banished it to my shelf where it remained untouched for the next four years.

This project functions, essentially, as a series of monologues between two very different people: myself, and my creation, Scott Benis. After considering how I wished to construct this piece, I decided that perhaps the most engaging means to discuss the experience of teaching in a rural school should operate more accord- ing to the conventions of a performance and reflect less the rhetoric typically associated with academic writing. Thus, rather than distance ourselves from our product and strip our voices of their emotional undercurrents—which, by exten- sion, would deny the piece genuine perspectives on what teachers actually *feel* while in the rural classroom—this narrative places emotions and thoughts center stage.

Intentionally blurring the lines between the accepted genres of autobiography and ethnography (the latter having its roots in the scientific methods of inquiry) is admittedly a risky maneuver, for in doing so the author risks replacing scholarship with superficiality and serious social issues with shameless self-aggrandizement. Yet I echo Ruth Behar (1996) in proclaiming that failure to acknowledge the validity of vulnerable writing stems from an unwillingness to accept that such writing might indeed lead the reader into a sea of social exploration. In this case, the emotional context for sharing rural teaching experiences (as well as recogniz- ing that in some capacity, all teaching contains a performative element) is para- mount, for without an acknowledgment of the emotional toll all schools—not simply rural schools—place upon teachers, these stories will, by default, lack any capacity for true resonance. Quite simply, teachers need to tell other teachers how they feel about teaching, and I feel as though I've structured this narrative in a manner conducive to achieving that particular end.

Again, the two voices present in this piece are those of Scott Benis—my 2008 literary counterpart—reconciling his artificial place as a stranger in a nonexistent rural land, and mine, four years detached from the creation of Scott and his ensu- ing struggles at South Dalesburg High School. In this piece, I seek to decipher the means by which Scott's story sheds light on my own real-life experience during my career's infancy as a rural high school teacher: to embrace the vulnerability of Scott's experience as a means of exploring his creation and what his journey yields about the anxieties I experienced as a new teacher penetrating the bound- aries of a rural environment and encountering the adolescent Other.

Everything in the "Then" sections comes directly from Scott's mind; presented, unabridged, as I transcribed it between November 2008 and April 2009. It's important to remember that what Scott thinks is what I *intended* him to think; the thoughts themselves were contrived as a means to motivate the progression of the novel and don't necessarily reflect what I, as the author, actually felt at the time. In other words, the text itself isn't nearly as important as the source of its inspiration: its existence justifying its examination. In the "Now" section, I attempt to reflect upon my past self's perceptions of Scott's new, rural environment as presented through the mind of my creation. Everything else, I believe, speaks for itself.

As the reader, you are now part of this process; by willing to engage in and with our stories, you've been cast, so to speak, in the performance, which will soon unfold. You'll quickly discover that this narrative contains no stage directions, nor does it always (or ever) present itself in the most linear fashion. The same can be said of teaching. As Scott and I learned soon after our immergence into the west-central Indiana corn fields, *real* teaching is anything but linear and never comes with stage directions. Yet, as with teaching, it is these imperfections of the human circumstance that most often leads to the most profound discoveries. We hope these stories yield such discoveries.

Then: The Dilemma

With the exception of about a three-mile stretch closer to my apartment, the road between my school and my apartment runs parallel to an old abandoned train track rusting about ten meters from the highway. Back when it was in operation, the track primarily transported wealthy passengers between Cincinnati and Chicago, but also ran longer trips down to St. Louis, and even as far west as San Francisco. They never built a train station between my school and my home. No one ever saw the need for one, I guess. The closest depot was located about thirty miles farther south of the school and, since the closing, has been converted into a nostalgic, train-themed diner that I hear serves really good hash browns. I'll have to check them out sometime.

The track closed about ten years after the Dalesburg County Jail was built, but during its infancy, I often wonder if inmates would gaze through their bars at the shiny metal cars speeding by and ask themselves who was riding inside of them: where they were going, and how long it would take to get there. I imagine they'd sit in their cells and hope that one day they too could hop a train out west and embark on a better life for themselves. The only thing the passengers aboard the trains ever saw when they rode past the town was wide open American country, full of potential, itching to be conquered: the manifestation of our national ideal. I don't think anyone ever saw the prison.

Now, as I approach the track crossing, I realize that stopping is pointless. I stand no chance of getting hit crossing these tracks. They're dead. Useless. The neglected byproducts of a foreign age. The trains and their wealthy passengers have moved elsewhere. Still, despite my prevailing rationality, I slow to a sliding stop just before the first rail, my tires slipping on the thin layer of ice covering the frozen gravel. As the sun begins to set over the horizon, I wonder what I'd be seeing if I was standing in this same spot 150 years ago. Everyone around here knows that thousands of people spent a portion of their lives—often sacrificing them along the way—building these tracks. America owes a hefty debt to the millions of man-hours put into the construction of our iron infrastructure. I can see them standing in front of me, wedging massive spikes in the ground and hammering them into the earth with the atavistic strength of self-made men: men who went home to families they loved and who loved them, and who lived off of the earnest living their patriarch provided. I imagine just how different the town must have looked back then as I sit in my car beside these empty tracks: the lone vehicle on this rural tangent of a chaotic nation. I was born a century too late.

But it gets me thinking. If I were alive 150 ago, would I have still been a teacher? What would I have taught? Would I have dedicated my life to pushing students to seek a better life for themselves? Could I have ever reconciled my desire for them to pursue greatness with the realization that this nation needs railroads and it needs men to build them? For every scholar I would have churned out, there'd be one less man to drive the spikes, one less mile of conquered America. Would I have been among them, working side-by-side, day in and day out, burning daylight until the moon's beams wrought their ghosts upon our brow as we built this country one link at a time? Would I have survived that life? Could I now?

Now: The Problem With Needing

One of the first obstacles I confronted in my rural school was the awkward con-flation of necessity and want. As a privileged college graduate—born and raised in an affluent suburb of north-side Indianapolis—I remember thinking that I had a firm grasp on what it meant to need something. Where I came from, people *needed* cars to go on dates. We *needed* money to spend on dates. We needed an edu-cation to get good jobs, and we needed good jobs so we could be happy with the families that we convinced ourselves we needed. We needed the Colts to win on Sundays so that they could make the playoffs, and we *needed* reservations otherwise we wouldn't get into the swanky Italian restaurant after the game.

We never needed food. We just always had it. We never needed new clothes because our old clothes were still pretty new anyway. My dad didn't need to work three shifts to pay for heat during the winter, and my mom never needed to bail him out of jail when he got caught selling drugs so he could pay for heat after getting laid off. Necessity, for a suburbanite like me, simply equated the perpetu-ation of luxury. Everything else was a given.

Now, of course my experience, albeit tainted by the blissful ignorance of youth, offers an overly romantic view of the suburbs, and paints an equally perilous view of life in the rural schools. This pejorative binary, for me, is not a source of pride. But it existed; and like it or not, I know that when I first stepped into my school, I did so with the horribly misguided tendency to define those kids as, to bor-row from Thomas Lux, "the people of the other village": I do this, they do that. Still, despite my greatest efforts to purge them, these perspectives on necessity informed my upbringing and thus governed my initial perspectives of my rural students.

My students *did* need heat. They *did* need food. They did need clothes to wear, and they needed someone to tell them how to wash those clothes. They needed stable homes, and solid floors, and parents with jobs, and a reason to say no to drugs. They needed these things because so many of my students simply didn't have them. For them, these things were not givens, but rather superfluous accents to an otherwise unfamiliar life.

What they didn't need, however, at least according to them, was literacy. They didn't need to know how to read. They didn't need to learn about Thomas Lux, or poetry, or how to write, or what prepositional phrases are, or why they're bad to end sentences with. My students would always claim they didn't need what I was selling because in their rural paradigm of farm culture, such arbitrary magic tricks weren't ever going to yield a crop. Semicolons don't make working the factory line any easier, and reading Whitman doesn't make you a better welder. What distinguished these kids, I feel, from my urban or suburban counterparts (with whom I had much more familiarity) isn't so much that they complained about learning English—lots of students hate Shakespeare—but that their disgust of school was predicated on them "knowing" exactly what they were going to do the second they graduated because they'd been doing it all their lives.

Most of my students learned to drive before the age of ten: again, out of necessity for working on the farm. They hunted. Whereas I had never seen a gun before in my life, save for on police officers or in sporting goods stores, these students were handling pistols, rifles, and shotguns since elementary school.

They were well versed in machinery. A shocking few ever had allergies. And my heart melted for each and every one of them. I loved those students, and I loved hearing about their lives and learning about their town, which was so different than anything I'd ever encountered. But when it came to teaching them Language Arts, we'd eventually encounter a chiasmus of sorts: a crisscrossing of our respective narratives. Where emphasis on one of our goals would go up, the other would decline. During my first year, I never could reconcile literacy's importance with the fact that these kids would rather be field-dressing the deer they killed earlier in the morning than read *The Leatherstocking Tales*. While I learned to recognize the validity of their career endeavors, I never managed to cater my teaching (and the corresponding state standards) to accommodate those pursuits.

Looking back, I still find it difficult to see the 'right' way of doing things. It wasn't as though my students' lack of academic interests was coupled with a passion for other material. They rarely expressed an interest in anything at all. As one student once told me, which is a sentiment echoed by several of his peers, "I just want to work in the factory every day and get drunk every night." Thus, when it came to certain material, I would remove my rural mask and reveal to my students the identity that I could never entirely conceal: that of a privileged white outsider, infiltrating their rural schoolhouse in an attempt to mold them into something they were not. Sure, I could say I wanted them all to pursue their dreams and work in the factory down the road, but I'm not sure anybody would have ever believed me. Four years later, I'm not sure I believe myself.

Then: The Betrayal of Place

A pristine brick archway accentuated with an open, wrought iron gate welcomes students, faculty, alumni, and other guests to Biltmore College's main entrance. The campus itself mirrors the same rigorous academic standards and architectural integrity honored by most prestigious American universities: statues of white men whose past accomplishments escape the cognizance of anyone who walks by, water fountains and copper benches donated by former graduating classes, hidden cobblestone alleys, and mythic tales of clock tower suicides and naked mile runs. The meticulous landscaping and eminent red brick buildings shield those present from the harsh realities that the once renowned land-grant school now sits at the epicenter of an impoverished hellhole: engulfed on all ends by urban crime, drugs, destitution, and a perpetual layer of smog thick enough to limit visibility to only three or four smoke stacks down the road. Walking under the monstrous phallic tower near the heart of campus, few would believe that just outside the private college's boundaries lurks perhaps the most menacing government subsidized residential blocks in the state. Biltmore prides itself on its tradition of promoting life on the brink of discovery. The residents of the nearby neighborhoods are just trying to stay alive.

Now: Locating the Self

Part of my frustration with teaching in a rural environment stemmed from my inability to locate that environment in any sort of specific context. I could never map my school in relation to anything else. Quite literally, it sits just off the shoulder of a highway and is surrounded by miles of cornfields: fairly typical, I would imagine, of many rural schools. Nevertheless, not having that proximal awareness of the school with regard to other places made it difficult, on a subconscious level, to justify working there. My failure to position the school (and all that that entails) into any sort of manageable capacity rendered me unable to contextualize myself in that environment. The school was in the middle of nowhere. By teaching there, I too became in the middle of nowhere. These anxieties would govern, to a certain extent, the duration of my employment.

In his book *Public Opinion*, Walter Lippman (1922) describes our collective inability to perceive and functionally interpret the external world. Because of this, Lippman argues, we create pseudo-environments—which by their nature are biased and fictional—in order to navigate the waters of our present circumstance. This makes it possible for people to actually live in the same world but process that world as if it were a different one. For me, the creation of Scott Benis served as a means to craft my own pseudo-environment: a place in which I could live, grow, and combat the nervous apprehensions that derived from my external world through the mind of someone entirely under my control. My school became South Dalesburg High School. I became Scott, and Scott became me.

Soon, my teaching became my theater: a creative outlet through which I could expel the myriad of tensions resulting from the demands of the job—demands for which I often felt unprepared and unqualified. My students became characters in my narrative and my colleagues, my fellow actors. Some days we performed comedies: other days, tragedies. Some days we'd have an off performance, which left the audience disgruntled through our failure to engage them. I maintained semblances of authenticity—albeit overshadowed by the guise of my performance—during that first year, but my presence in the building was more often than not governed by an impulse to be somewhere else. I played my part well, pouring my heart into the role, but at the end of the day, I always got in my car and returned to my life.

My real self was elsewhere, in the city: detached from the persona that existed in the classroom. My wife and I lived in a college town located in a different county from where I taught. No aspect of my schooled-self followed me home at night, thus allowing me to completely strip myself of any attachment I had to the building or my students. I lived on campus. I worked in the corn. As my distain for the monotony of the daily drive to the country increased, so too did the sense of contrived nostalgia for my surrounding academic community. I began to long for a place that never existed, but nonetheless a place in which I had spent the better part of a decade living.

Over time, my real collegiate community evolved into a pseudo-environment of its own: my home becoming a counter-creation to the narrative I had constructed around my school. I would go to my college's football games, don myself in its spirit wear, converse with my former professors, and dine at the multitude of campus restaurants. Occasionally, I would even drive to campus at night and meander through the old buildings and perch myself atop one of the stone benches, mimicking the same path from when I was student nearly a decade prior. But I wasn't a student anymore. I just lived there and acted as one. As a teacher, my presence on campus was no less performative than my presence in the classroom. I was untethered to any particular community, the anchors I once had at home having been lifted by my refusal to accept what that home had become. I was no longer a college student driving to the country to student teach; I was a rural teacher who lived on a college campus. I failed to locate myself in any particular community. As a result, I failed to locate myself at all. My only consolation was the fact that I still had my stories: the ones I taught in school and the ones I created for my life.

Then: The Betrayal of People

The last I heard, Lee Marshall—my former professor and mentor who abandoned his graduate student cohort following a fallout with members of the senior faculty—was working in Boston as a whale-watching tour guide. He'll grow old at sea, and I've no doubt the salt of the ocean will turn his beard grey, and his skin the beating sun will make leathery and calloused like the heroes of the books he once taught at that school so long ago. One day he'll have a passenger, a naïve mainlander, wearing a Biltmore sweatshirt. After winning the lad over with his usual yarns of mystery and nautical adventure, Lee will mock the boy's choice of schools and insist, instead, that in the sea dwells the source of all learning. The boy will return home, attend his classes, and near graduation, having never severed the memories of that grizzled old Boston man. He'll quit school to embark on a career on the water, giving tours to rich people in college sweatshirts and eliciting genuine laughter at true stories he just made up. Years later, the boy, now a grizzled old man himself, will regret not finishing school, but the burdens of family and life will prove too great to anchor and return. Thus, like Lee himself, the legacy of my former hero will forever remain that of perpetual isolation from the realisms of the world: always floating just off the shore of rationality. I am no exception.

Now: Self-Defiance

It took about six months for it to happen. I felt betrayed. I felt they lied to me. Everybody. As if they were all part of the same sick, perpetual joke. All of them. Laughing at my expense. I felt betrayed by the students for not being as eager to learn as everybody said they'd be. I felt betrayed by my teachers who told me that the students would be eager to learn. I felt betrayed by my parents for never pushing me to do just one thing, and I felt betrayed by my university for stressing that I should specialize in just one thing. I felt betrayed by my professors for giving me a Master's degree and then encouraging me to teach high school. I felt betrayed by my literary heroes—the American Transcendentalists who wrote of living life deliberately in the woods, but then abandoned their cabins to return to the city when life got tough. I felt betrayed by the people who taught me to love what these writers wrote. *Walden* is a sham. Thoreau was just a rich kid, playing house by a pond.

I felt betrayed by the cities for not supporting the people in the country, and I felt betrayed by the country for not striving to live in the city. I felt betrayed by the nation for not recognizing the actual needs of its students, and I felt betrayed by the students for not standing up for what they needed. I felt betrayed by society for not taking teachers seriously, and I felt betrayed by teachers who didn't take society seriously. I felt betrayed by my car for not breaking down on the way to work, and I felt betrayed by my school for not paying me mileage. I felt betrayed by my students' parents for not being better, and I felt betrayed by my hometown for teaching me to be prejudiced against the poor. I didn't know these people, but I convinced myself that I did so I could sleep at night. I felt betrayed by myself for not being able to get over myself.

Then: Where I Worked, and What I Worked For

Bogle is a broken town, the weathered remnants of which typically blanket late-night commercials imploring viewers to donate money or canned foods: simply another fractured shell of twentieth-century economic prosperity and industrial hubris. Every morning, the 53 seconds it takes to speed through the town at a cool 41 miles per hour always makes me grateful that I came from a house that wasn't across the street from the courthouse/liquor store: that I came from a place where businesses didn't specialize in selling discount jewelry, insurance, AND funeral plots. That my town didn't sell hunting ammunition in hospital lobbies, and that at 7:15 in the middle of a January morning, old men didn't meander through the middle of the roads looking for loose change.

By contrast, seven miles down the road, the town of Ignatius serves as the residence for the more upscale of Dalesburg County citizens. The student body of South Dales consists of roughly 40 percent Bogle residents and 40 percent Ignatius residents, with the remainder hailing from other, more ascetically deficient smaller surrounding towns. Like Bogle, Ignatius was founded primarily on the basis of agriculture, but unlike Bogle, it doesn't appear to be hit nearly as hard by the disappearance of the numerous industrial plants. In fact, in the last decade or so, Ignatius has boomed into one of the fastest growing towns in Dalesburg County. Some people are even beginning to call it a city, but several locals are disputing the suggested nomenclature, maintaining that, "Cities is where the devil is."

Watching the sun rise to my left every morning—as cliché as it sounds—actually used to invigorate me for the entire day. With a smile on my face, I would prepare myself for the myriad of engaging lessons I would bestow upon my students: oh, the young minds that I would undoubtedly mold with my superior intellect and keen insights into the adolescent psyche. I welcomed the arrival of the Bogles and the Ignatiuses on my journey as I paid homage to the little people of the world: those hard-working Americans who put meat on my plate and milk in my cup. Back in the fall, I felt that this drive would lead me to some sort of greater purpose—that I was actually doing something with my life. That all my training and skills and passions and knowledge would finally reach an audience. In the fall, when Principal Avery Thicke welcomed me aboard the faculty of South Dalesburg High School, I was happy. I had arrived.

But as the weeks turned to months, the sun began to refrain from its spritely ritual of illuminating the horizon with its glowing, celestial dance. The road gradually grew darker, the world colder and far less personal. All intimacy of the drive soon vanished as I found myself entombed beneath the bleakness of Bogle and Ignatius. I quickly gained an uncomfortable familiarity with every dust-covered storefront windowpane. I knew every pothole, every mailbox, every abandoned car and boarded house and severed tree limb and out-of-place children's playground and stray mitten and bald tire filling the ditches on the side of the road. No longer was I merely an innocent passerby headed toward a brighter and more promising tomorrow. I was Ignatius. I became Bogle. I began to see my future in the old, shoeless man in the middle of the road, as each trip through town signified one step closer to the strangling truth of permanence.

Now: The Betrayal of Initiation

When you get your teaching license, it doesn't come with a community membership card. And why should it? The idea is that with the license, you should be qualified to teach at any school that has an opening. And so, without hesitation, we apply for jobs based on their vague, standardized Internet postings, and we go to interviews and make our cover letters look all nice and formal because we think that each school is the same. Put me in the city; put me in the country—it doesn't matter. I am who I am and that's what they're going to get. Thinking otherwise risks accusations of being racist, classist, elitist, or any other kind of 'ist' that our culture so vehemently condemns. But schools are not the same. And teaching in a rural environment necessitates membership, in some capacity, in that particular community.

I was always an outsider in my school. Geographically, I didn't live in the county, so my immigrant status rendered certain material more difficult to teach for me than for my local colleagues, several of whom sold their nicer houses in neighboring counties so that they could live down the street from the school. It wasn't simply the convenience of proximity that prompted the move; it was the expectation that, like the parochial schools of old, teachers maintain a positive communal visibility at all times. While Washington Irving certainly painted a negative picture of parochialism in the nineteenth century, in a way, my presence in the building was never too unlike an Irving narrative: a contemporary Ichabod Crane riding into town on his horse (I wish it were a Mustang, but really it was Honda), penetrating the perimeters of the tightly stitched rural fabric and exposing the villagers to the toxins of outside thinking. The fear there, of course, is, as Kurt Vonnegut (2000) notes with regards to writing, "If you open a window and make love to the world, so to speak, your story will get pneumonia." I feared I was the carrier for an infection that could spread through the entire community.

As an outsider, I had an acute awareness of the threat my teaching posed: not necessarily because of what I taught or even how I taught it, but because it was being taught by someone who would never be seen taking communion at the county church. The parents of the community would never know my wife from little league games, and I would never coach their kids during the summer. My children would never go to the district schools, and I would never bump into one of my students at the supermarket while weighing the pros and cons of buying organic squash. With the exception of back-to-school night (an event attended by roughly 20 percent of the parent cohort), my presence in the building never manifested as more than a name. Parents never saw me. They didn't talk to me. They didn't know how I old I was, or where I grew up, or how I dressed every day, or if I bathed regularly, or if my socks matched, or if I believed in Jesus.

Granted, by and large, my name was associated with effective teaching and a respect by the students. But outside the school, it was still simply a name: a malleable construct of arbitrary symbols molded to fit the needs of any given moment. Inside the building, I was Ichabod Crane: the learned, naïve, bibliophilic intruder. Within the greater community however, because my capacity as a member functioned solely within the confines of the school's faculty, I feared I would be seen as more of a legend with which the town was forced to reconcile its entrenched anxieties: the Headless Horseman in today's Sleepy Hollow. While over time my success as a teacher and strong, positive rapport with the students alleviated some of the tensions surrounding my outsider status, I can never discard them entirely. If only I had a membership card.

Once initiated, members of rural communities, by nature of their admission into the network, have the luxury of being dealt with rather than dismissed. People forget names, banishing them from the communal lexicon. It's harder to forget faces. It's even more difficult to forget a name that's attached to a face that lives next door and borrows sugar on Fridays to make pies on Saturdays for the dinner on Sundays. Inevitably, with membership comes attachment, thus making it all the more difficult to sever those ties with which we've forged an intrinsic bond. Yes, people move houses, change jobs, and die. But if someone exists only as a name, then they were never really alive in the first place.

Then: The Burden of Routine

One of the school's janitors is emptying the wastebaskets in the main hallway. I think his name is Ed. He looks like an Ed. Like a man who's been doing the same job for the better part of a quarter century, he envelopes the edges of the can with his oversized plastic bag with one arm and pours the receptacle's contents into his personal janitor's cart with the other. He moves deliberately down the hallway to the next trashcan and repeats the motions. This is his job. Picking up the garbage. I notice a wedding ring on his finger; what first draws my attention to it is the fact the majority of his fingers are coated with the thick, soot-covered calluses only a life sweeping up dirty floors can provide. The ring is the only thing that shines. The ring and his brilliant nametag. Ed. The luster of his ring suggests that he sometimes removes it at work, perhaps out of fear that he'll tarnish it. Or maybe he just wants the ladies to think he's single. Oh, Ed. You're still married even if you're not wearing your ring. Taking it off doesn't change who you are.

Still, despite the certain leathery quality his callused hands otherwise possess, there is a quiet, bucolic strength to the man that I'm seeing for the first time in the dimly lit, eerily silent hallway. I start to grow envious of the humble public servant as I stand but six or seven feet from the Colony's entrance. You can't outsource people like Ed. There's always trash that needs to be picked up.

I've never heard him say anything to anyone, probably because he's one of the only janitors here who speaks English. In fact, I probably wouldn't even know him at all except he was recognized earlier in the year for his 25 years of loyal dedication to the South Dalesburg Community School System. His kids were at the celebration. They didn't say much either: merely stood in the back and waited for the rest of the staff to devour Ed's cake before helping themselves to a sliver. The superintendent gave their father a nice plaque. His wife cried. He looked uncomfortable. I sensed he wasn't used to wearing ties. I think he missed his mop. I remember feeling sorry for him at the time: happy for his accomplishment, but inwardly bemoaning the fact that while everyone present at the party appeared very appreciative of the man's unrelenting service, without hesitation, they'd insist he replace a light bulb in their classroom the instant it went out instead of recognizing that perhaps the man—he is a man, after all—may have more important issues to worry about than whether or not his elitist colleagues could show their class the cool PowerPoint presentation they stole from the Internet about Hamlet. Still, day in and day out, Ed roams the halls of South Dalesburg, reading disregarded student notes and mopping up spilled milk. Despite my agony and unrelenting desire to do so, I doubt Ed's ever cried once.

Now: Today's Sisyphus

I was the first person in my family to graduate from my high school. My father graduated from an all-boys Catholic school in Indianapolis, and my mother's all-girls school no longer exists, having merged with another all-boys institution sometime during the Reagan years. Aside from my brother, no other member of my family—immediate or extended—will graduate from my suburban high school.

My rural students could never relate.

As the yearbook advisor, I was privy to an abundance of school artifacts and community memorabilia: old letter-jackets, faded photos of past graduating classes—odd wooden buckets that I'm told had some special value to the athletic department—and every yearbook the school ever published. Every so often, on days when we'd completed our respective publication tasks, a typical recreational activity would be to peruse the old yearbooks for pictures of my students' family members. To my initial shock, not only did the majority of my kids have parents who both graduated from the school, but in extended ways, many of my students were related to one another. Half brothers, stepsisters, cousins, uncles, and in-laws; the interwoven network of familial relations immediately caught me off guard, as I hailed from a city where I never met a single person whose parents graduated from our school.

I don't mean to suggest that any of these relationships were incestuous in nature. Such stereotypes, I feel, often plague depictions of rural American culture, and were certainly not the case here. Rather, it was evident that I worked in a community where people simply didn't leave; instead people got married, had kids, got divorced, got remarried, had more kids who then had kids with other people who recently migrated to the area—and the cycle continued. It's just how it was; and from what I could gather, it's how it always had been.

So the degree to which tradition and routine governed the communal impulses of the town often proved problematic, particularly in a Language Arts classroom where an outsider was attempting to teach things like Camus' notions of the absurd: a philosophical critique of the futility and ultimate despair of daily, mechanized existence. How do I comment on the absurdity of factory work in a room filled with future factory workers? How do I help students negotiate a consciousness of the absurdities of their lives—which Camus would argue ultimately leads to liberation—without risking the development of more absurdities? While I've written on these issues above with regard to students' perception of necessity, when married to the idea of tradition, the resistance to such material—and the struggle to navigate my own pedagogical approach—proved all the greater.

Over time, as a result of more than simply teaching Camus, I grew to acknowledge the absurdities of my teacher experience: absurdities not unique to rural settings, but pervasive in all contemporary classrooms. I became Sisyphus, pushing my own rock up that infernal hill. Whether or not I made it to the top was of no consequence; the rock always fell back down the hill, and I would have to retrieve it. Standardized tests, parental apathy, colleague fatigue, disciplinary inconsistencies, lack of public support, and all the other bullets on the typical list of Why-Teachers-Quit questionnaires—each was its own rock impeding the ascension of my career's summit. According to Camus, recognizing the absurd leads to freedom; but when the machine enters the garden and proceeds to mechanize everything whose organic and fluid essence you've held dear and true for the entirety of your existence, it's hard to imagine Sisyphus happy. The hill never plateaus, but the buses still arrive every morning.

Then: The Cartographer's Fallacy

When I tell people what I do for a living—people who flock in mirrored social circles as my parents and other grad school friends—I'm often bombarded with the most smug expressions of condolence: rueful sighs and misty eyes that would otherwise weep for my tragic shortcomings, were it not a faux pas for them to lament my vocation in public. So you're a teacher? Where? Oh, you don't actually teach? You work in the—oh—well at least it's a job! At first it bothered me. I worried I was becoming the guy in every family who falls drastically short of the ideals for which the family has so proudly stood since the beginning of civilized time. I feared I embarrassed my parents, and that they would rather lie and say I was a principal than tell the truth and say I'm actually a glorified prison guard. And with each stuffy party or overpriced soiree, I grew more and more convinced that I am yet another victim of the world's discrimination: the poster boy for why children should stay in school and never settle for anything less than their dreams. You don't want to end up like Scott Benis, honey. Eat your vegetables.

But I'm not a teacher. That's not who I am. I teach high school because I don't really know who I am. Oh, what subject do you teach? Well, I'm licensed to teach English. Usually that's enough. It's the most truth I'm willing to divulge to people who I feel don't really have an investment in my career. No one cares what you do for a living. They ask because they think they have to. They ask because they think that knowing what I do will tell them who I am. When I say I have an English license, they can put me in a category in very much the same fashion all people do when they attempt to reconcile the untenable facets of the external world with their incessant desire to understand that very world. It's why explorers make maps and why racists hate races. Our quest for certainty eclipses our awareness of subjectivity. He's a teacher. Scott Benis is a teacher. I've known teachers before, thus I know Scott Benis. And, thus, I feel sorry for him. They don't understand that this was a choice. This whole thing happened because I wanted it to. It's a choice.

I only wish I had another one.

"Have a good weekend, Mr. Benis."

"You too," I offer over my shoulder, though I don't turn around to see who said it. It doesn't really matter anyway. It was a student. That's all I really know. Like the thousands before it and the hordes still to come, it was only a student. I slide past the clusters of eager weekenders and head to my car before the buses block the exit of the parking lot. A few more students tell me to have a good weekend. I say nothing in return. But of course I make sure to smile and nod. I wouldn't want to be rude.

Curtain Call: The Monomythic Teacher

I went to the corn, not because I wanted to live deliberately or to suck out all the marrow of life, but because, having basked in the liberating sanctity of a formal education, I wished to share life's marrow with my students: coating their innocent, adolescent fronts with regurgitated remnants of lessons *I* loved, material *I* wanted to teach, issues that *I* considered the most vital for a deliberate and sublime existence. Ironically, when I came to leave, I discovered that I had not lived. I lived a life that was not life. I practiced resignation, all in the spirit of denying my rural environment a reality to which it was rightfully entitled: a *real* place with *real* students who needed *real* teachers to teach them. Like Thoreau's (2012) *Walden*, I intended during the time at my rural school to 'conduct an experiment.' Yet the more I treated my students as subjects during my first year, the more I homogenized their Otherness, and by extension stripped them of their subjectivities. As I internalized the betrayal I perceived to have originated from the outside, the more I became myself, a betrayer of the pedagogical imperatives for which I was hired. I put on a good show, but the resonating sounds of disembodied hands applauding from the house served as a greater impetus for perseverance than the bodies themselves.

I now return to begin again from the ending. In a way, I consider myself a perversion of the Campbellian monomyth: refusing to identify as a hero but recognizing that I've returned to the realm of the common day and must now accept it as real. I've lived in two very different worlds and have crafted two very different identities in order to combat the inherent obstacles within. Following the return of his hero, Campbell (2008) writes, "He no longer tries to live but willingly relaxes to whatever may come to pass in him; he becomes, that is to say, an anonymity" (p. 205). But the hero isn't the only one whose anonymity forms through the crossing of borders, worlds, or tracks.

In every rural community, the cries of a thousand faces remain unanswered. We sneeze through their towns, dine in their shops, and pump in their gas. Then we leave. By the time I decided to depart from my rural school to light out for my own territory, I had finally reconciled my initial reservations about crossing over to the other side of the tracks. These weren't just students; they were *my* students, and membership card or not, I tried my best to fight for them. After four years in the building, I realized, tracks don't spring up naturally. We create them: forging them through our manifest destiny to conquer, divide, and abandon. So, before my memories of teaching in a rural school banished into obscurity, I wanted to resurrect Scott Benis, if for no other reason than to remind myself, as I sit in my urban home down the street from my college town, that in another life, a different version of myself rode into the American pastoral in my Honda and taught a bunch of farmers about a man named Al Camus. We studied Thomas Lux not as people of other villages but, for a threadbare patch in the fabric of time, as members of the same community. We did this. We did that.

We learned about a cabin on a pond and watched movies about the American Teen. The kids in those movies didn't look like my students, though. They lived in the city and dressed differently and talked differently and thought differently than my kids. No better, no worse. Just different. We watched and listened to their stories, and the whole time, I sat at my desk, just as I sit now in my urban office, looking out my window at the train speeding by, and I thought to myself: What stories are those kids going to tell, and who's going to listen to them?

References

Behar, R. (1996). *The vulnerable observer: Anthropology that will break your heart.* New York, NY: Beacon Press.

Campbell, J. (2008). *The hero with a thousand faces: The collected works of Joseph Campbell* (3rd ed.). New York, NY: New World Publishing.

Camus, A. (1991). *The myth of Sisyphus: And other essays* (Reissue ed.). New York, NY: Vintage.

Lippman, W. (1922). *Public opinion.* New York, NY: Harcourt, Brace and Company.

Mutter, S. (1992). *Surrational images: Photomontage.* Chicago, IL: University of Illinois Press.

Thoreau, H. D. (2012). *Walden.* New York, NY: Empire Books.

Vonnegut, K. (2000). *Bagombo snuff box: Uncollected short fiction* (Reissue ed.). Berkley, CA: Berkley Trade.

5

FALLING THROUGH THE RABBIT HOLE AND TEACHING THROUGH THE LOOKING GLASS

Experiences of a New Teacher in a Rural School

Kendra McPheeters-Neal

LOWELL HIGH SCHOOL, LOWELL, INDIANA

Somewhere along my 43-mile commute, I drove through the looking glass. Despite having a quality education and student teaching at a prestigious high school, I was unprepared for my first job as an English teacher in rural West Central Indiana. Everything—the community's and students' views of education, the knowledge base, and in some respects even the language—seemed to be the opposite of familiar suburbia.

In college, I was prepared for every educational environment, or so I thought, through various pre-service practicum experiences alongside my classes. We considered the highly prized, rich, suburban school as well as its antithesis. We discussed the possibility of being in this 'other' environment—of having little funding and support, few books, and students who would know just by looking at us that we were alien. This scenario was primarily shared in the context of being an inner-city school, an urban school in which many of the students grew up believing that they were incapable of rising above their current circumstances. I prepared myself for the possibility of teaching in a school like this; I did not realize that I would have to restructure the parameters of my thinking to include Farmville, USA.

I never truly considered the environment in which I felt myself best suited to work in the months after graduating in May of 2010. I applied to any school in Indiana that had an opening for English and interviewed at ten schools ranging from urban to rural, public to private, and on-track to well behind state standards. For my ninth interview, I drove to a corporation taking up what appeared to be the size of an average cornfield. I was hopeful; the principal did not mention coaching in our initial conversation. During my interview, while trying not to stare at the stuffed falcon behind the principal's head, I answered questions as to how I would accommodate students who were behind grade-level, what leadership skills I had gained in college, how I would differentiate education, and if I were comfortable with tutoring in math and science. I related how holding multiple offices with Purdue's fencing club and working as a coaching assistant for one of the best high school debate teams in the state gave me relatable experience working with young adults and being in a position of authority, how I actually tested better in math and science than in English, and how nine years of tutoring experience made it easy for me to individualize lessons. Looking back, none of these things prepared me for working with many students who were not only behind academically, but who also held a frighteningly archaic view of education—specifically, that education stopped as soon as their fingers grasped their diplomas. Upon receiving a call from the school's principal, I patiently waited for the "We appreciated interviewing you, but . . . " I had heard eight times before. Instead I was offered a position on July 10, 2010, as a freshman English and basic skills teacher.

The day I drove to my new workplace to get my keys, I canceled an interview with one of the most prominent suburban schools in the state, partly due to a desire to avoid Indianapolis commuter traffic and partly due to curiosity begging me to try a small school with a four-person English team that was bound to be a more intimate department setting. As I pranced into the building, I could barely contain my excitement. I looked forward to receiving the same type of organized curricula to mold into my own that I had been given at the school in which I had student taught. Instead I was given my key, which I had to fight to make function; my classroom, which was still filled with the previous occupant's belongings and looked like a prison cell; and a sad smirk from my assistant principal after asking her if there was a set curriculum for English courses. Not only would I have no curriculum map or syllabus, there was also no record of which novels were traditionally taught at the freshman level. The only tangible item to help me plan an entire year's worth of lessons was a battered teacher's edition of the 2002 literature textbook used in Indiana—the same textbook that I had used my freshman year of high school. I asked the vice-principal if this was a textbook adoption year for English. She told me that the English year had already passed, and the staff had opted not to renew in order to save funds (and keep from having to restructure their lessons around changing materials). Soon after, I transferred the student copies of the book into my classroom from cabinets in my department head's room, noting how many penises were drawn along the edges of the books and on their pages, wondering if that weird gooey mess was gum or strawberry jelly, and counting how many were practically falling apart. I was not in my university city anymore where an entire room had been devoted to the meticulous keeping of the English department's textbooks and novels.

For the rest of the summer, I spent lunch breaks at my daycare job thumbing through the pages of the freshman literature text, grouping individual pieces into units and writing what activities could be done with each of them. By the end of the summer I had compiled a semester's worth of activities to be used with the literature tome, in addition to vague unit plans I composed about writing in different genres and reading John Knowles' *A Separate Peace*, a text that I had read in my own freshman class. I neglected the fact that I had been in honors and that this school did not track, a concept of which I needed reminding with some regularity. After having taught classes during student teaching composed entirely of four-year-college-bound students whose intrinsic motivations were enough to keep them on task, teaching students who did not care, who lacked rudimentary skills needed to begin a lesson, or who gave up or lost attention easily was by far the most difficult challenge I faced in both of my years at my rural school.

A few more days were spent in the classroom boxing up the former occupant's things to have moved to that teacher's new room, as well as e-mailing my department in order to learn which novels were typically taught in which classes. Through e-mail, I could infer that the department was fragmented; no one really spoke to one another about what they would teach, how they should teach it, and what skills needed to be covered before students could progress to the next grade-level. Furthermore, I was flabbergasted by the lack of choices in literature left for freshman English, the lack of options that the school possessed, and the small number of copies of each book—to the point where I would not be able to assign reading homework because there would not be enough copies for the whopping freshman class of 53 students. This was in part due to the attitudes of some of my former colleagues. Some teachers cautioned me against giving homework ("It will never come back to you"), teaching novels ("They'll never read them"), and attempting essays ("They plagiarize everything"). I was Alice getting to the far hill of my new classroom, being told to do the opposite of my beliefs to reach my students. Before I began, I was already feeling beaten.

Sadly, my defeatist attitude kept rearing its head in the days shortly before and during my first few days of teaching. Because I had classes of over 30 students in English and needed numerous computers for my basic skills classes, I realized shortly before school started that I would have to traverse between two classrooms on opposite ends of the school each passing period. Before classes started on my first teaching day, I was also told that because of a scheduling snafu, I would be losing one of my sections of basic skills and would pick up a section of eighth graders the next day. I had absolutely no preparation, no desire to teach junior high, and no choice. I smiled and said I was grateful even though feelings of dread and failure were already rising in my gut. That same day students were all introduced to me not by my smiling face pointing them in the direction of the seating chart, but rather by a sign in my scrawling cursive taped to the door, stating, "Welcome to Miss McPheeters' class! I will be here to open the door momentarily. Please wait patiently in the meantime." As I approached the garden of camouflage and tiny tees milling about my classroom door, I felt like Alice among the flowers having her petals scrutinized. My students were shocked by my youthful face and my articulation. Multiple students that first day asked me if I was from England, to which I laughed until I realized that they were entirely serious. I pronounced all of my syllables, did not employ double negatives, and avoided the word 'ain't.'

To my students, I may as well have been from England, or Mars for that matter. They spelled 'think' as 'thank,' thought the politically correct term for a black person was 'colored,' and had no desire to learn from someone who seemed to have nothing in common with their (in my initial, prejudiced assessment) backwoods ways. I had to find a way to reach my students in order to gain their respect and show that we had a common ground.

Within the first week, I realized that my 10-year membership in 4-H (even though I focused on crafts, rockets, and small animals as opposed to the more farm-centered projects) and my childhood of fishing with my grandfather and riding ATVs would help my students realize that we do come from at least minimally similar experiences. I stopped wearing jewelry and more business-type suits and skirts in favor of cardigans and slacks. I wore less clothing from higher end stores and more from typical teen and twenty-something locales, and my girls loved stating from which stores my clothes had come and if they had tried on that piece the last time they were at the mall that was 40 minutes from their town. While this provided an introduction into the ways in which we were similar, it wasn't until we were over a month into the school year that I finally began to reach my students.

In that first month of school, I learned very quickly that the lesson plans I had written as a review for junior high English were concepts that had never been taught. After grading the first one-page paper that my students were assigned over a person whose life they wished to emulate, I noticed that more papers had been plagiarized than had not. There were still hyperlinks from Wikipedia, despite an entire class period devoted to identifying when something is plagiarism as well as multiple days learning how to incorporate sources into a paragraph and how to write basic citations. After that first month, I had covered just over a week's worth of my initial lessons and was ready to start our discrimination unit—admittedly, a bold move that probably should have waited until later in the year, but one that I was hoping to align with September 11th. The lessons were going well; students were shocked and outraged by the poem "Ballad of Birmingham" because they did not understand why anyone would bomb a church, especially one with children in it, regardless of what color they happened to be. I was proud of my students for being so open-minded and adapting to correct terms for race. Just shy of a week into the unit, however, a student said the n-word in my class. This was the first big test of teaching for me, bigger than the plagiarism and paper rewriting or having to build a syllabus from scratch in a day. Instead of losing my temper and sending the student to the office, which I would have expected me to do, I closed my classroom door for one of the very few times in my two years at my school.

"How many of you think that word is okay to say?" A few students raised their hands, citing the fact that black people say it, that they heard it in their music all the time, and that the inoffensive version ended with *a* instead of *er*. Some, however, still believed the initial pejorative was perfectly usable. I was surprised for multiple reasons. First, I had no idea that I would be dealing with a cultural climate that contained members who would openly state that those types of slurs were not inappropriate and who felt that a word that could empower black culture was acceptable for them—29 white students, one half-Native American student, and one quarter-Japanese student—to use. Second, I was ashamed of myself because I mistakenly assumed that my students would listen to stereotypical country music, and I felt awful to have made that judgment. In that moment I realized that I was just as prejudiced as my students; the only difference was that my prejudice encompassed geographical location and socioeconomic status instead of race. This realization coupled with the derogatory word blurted by a student who thought it would be funny to say started the class that probably should have got me fired. I told my students to put on their adult helmets, because this could be a bumpy lesson.

I explained the history of the word. I explained the idea of taking back a horrible, derogatory word for empowerment. To demonstrate this, we first thought of something as simple as a student accepting and owning a nickname that originated as a sleight. We came up with examples, some of which were insightful and others which were downright insulting. Then I explained how something as degrading as the n-word being used by the people it was intended to hurt can be seen as taking the sting out of the word, making it powerless. And then I used a word of which I knew they would understand the gravity: the c-word. I said it. My students sat silently, un-mockingly, beautifully engaged as I thought to myself, "Getting fired this soon has to be a record, but if I get them to understand this, it will be worth it." We discussed how girls calling their girlfriends insulting names is seen by some feminists as empowering themselves while others see it as degradation. We took sides. We shared opinions and grew. Then we transferred those same thoughts to the n-word, a context that this Wonder Bread school had difficulty understanding until we used words with whose connotations they were familiar. None of us wanted to leave when the bell rang.

This lesson took place on a Friday. I spent the weekend in fear of how many parent voicemails would be waiting for me, chewing me out for the attempt at indoctrinating their children and saying such a foul word in the classroom. I checked my school e-mail every few hours hoping not to see an e-mail from my principal asking me to see him in his office first thing Monday morning. Not only was the next Monday eerily devoid of backlash, but my students and I had a deeper respect for one another. I started class by stating—and they readily accepted—that we had to learn the basics of reading, writing, speaking, and analyzing in order to progress to the more difficult subject matter like we had covered in the last class. I learned that this particular group of students thrived best on discussion and debate and began incorporating more speaking into the classroom.

While this anecdote seems to show the best that teaching can give—acquisition of knowledge, open-mindedness, challenging prior opinions and ideas, and the collective growth of a class who took charge of their own learning and participation—there were many more days that made it a challenge for me to want to keep teaching just within this unit. Soon after our initial discussion of the n-word, a student said in class that he was fine with 'them' so long as nobody in his family ever decided to date or marry one. Students said candidly that there was "a difference between black people and niggers." That initial discussion that seemed like such a milestone, a made-for-TV-movie perfect scene was only a tiny pebble thrown into the placid lake of their racism. My school is not singular in this respect. In a student interview done by Groenke and Nespor (2010), a student the same age as mine summarizes their mindset when he says, "As far as I'm concerned and I'll tell any of the teachers here, if they don't want to hear the word they don't need to come down to Rivertown because Rivertown is just 99.9 percent rednecks and everybody, nobody around here likes black people. That's why we've got like a total of three black people in our entire school" (p. 65). Though this may seem extreme, the demographics between Rivertown, Texas, and my rural school were remarkably similar, as was the sentiment expressed. The lack of exposure and stereotypes ingrained in my students from birth made breaking down any sort of racial barriers incredibly difficult—and left me as a first-year teacher wondering if it was even my place to try.

This was not the only occasion that caused me to question my choice in teaching location, as well as my career in general. Freshmen not knowing their parts of speech, what makes a sentence complete, or how to engage in reading kept me ripping out my hair. An eighteen-person eighth grade class half-filled with students at least four grades below level and half-filled with students who needed to be challenged beyond the typical eighth grade lesson kept me running in circles attempting to differentiate education as a first-year teacher. And lack of basic skills had me tutoring students in all of their classes, tracking all of their grades and missing assignments every day, and remediating in both English and math. I was competent enough, but in my frazzled state I felt inadequate, and each day seemed to bring a new failure on my part. I never seemed able to accurately gauge my students' level of prior knowledge, and things that I assumed were self-explanatory to eighth graders and freshmen were concepts that needed class time to clarify. During the introductory lesson to *The Diary of a Young Girl*, an eighth grader asked, "Jews worship Buddha, right?" I stopped midsentence to clarify what I had assumed would be common knowledge. After this fiasco, I quickly learned to supplement units with more in-depth study of their time periods. For *Romeo and Juliet*, my freshmen engaged in a side project a la 'Choose Your Own Adventure' novels in which they were given a social class and asked to respond to scenarios common to this socioeconomic status once a week. We then shared these situations and responses, analyzing assumptions and stereotypes, and how they were reflected in the play. This was the first unit in which I earned the praise of certain colleagues who were inspired by the novelty of my lessons and who gave me one of the best compliments I could receive—that my students were talking about the assignments in their other classes with excitement instead of resentment.

On more than one occasion, I recognized too late that I had inadvertently insulted students or asked them to imagine concepts that seemed a world away to me, having grown up in a supportive and loving home, but were everyday occurrences for them. The worst moment for me came during my teaching of *Romeo and Juliet*. My students read the scenes aloud, and then we would stop to piece together what had transpired. After Juliet's father disowned and insulted his daughter, my students looked at me dumbfounded. They should have been alarmed and outraged! We muddled through the happenings of the scene, and then I asked them how they would feel if their parents told them that they did not claim them as their children and called them terrible names. A few weak hands raised halfheartedly, small voices muttering, "That has happened to me." I wanted nothing more than to simultaneously hug those students and melt into a puddle of shame onto the carpet, avoiding a room of eyes that could see each emotional reaction pass over my face. At that time, I sincerely believed my students would be better served by a teacher who could empathize with their backgrounds.

To top it off, at that point I began learning more about the community than I think I was ready to know. There were certain students who refused to show me any respect, I discovered, simply because I was female, and women should not be working. I had my glasses knocked from my face by a student who had never been taught at home that it was inappropriate. When I became stern with a student for making him wait for assistance until I had gone through a problem with another student in basic skills, I was asked if I was on my period (and even after returning from the office and having a chat with me, he still did not see why his question was disrespectful). I was cussed out and had students get in my face and scream at me. This type of behavior was not unusual for a young, female teacher to encounter, especially by older, male students at my school. On the flipside of this coin, male students also asked me to dances and attempted to flirt with me and neither saw the disrespect nor the inappropriateness of these actions.

Thankfully, I had a very supportive administration that helped me tremendously through my first year of school. Some of the more overbearing students in my basic skills classes were switched to the other (read: older, male) basic skills instructor in the hopes that those students would respect him more due to his age and gender. A special needs teacher worked in inclusion in two of my classes. I knew how inclusion was supposed to work and was relieved that I would have an extra instructor to help me differentiate lessons. At my school, however, I believe this practice was little more than having another adult presence in the room for my two most behaviorally difficult classes, as the special needs teacher did little more than supervise students during instruction. As a teacher who had never encountered true behavioral issues, I still welcomed the extra support. As I gained knowledge about the culture of the community, I discovered a terrifying disparity in how the same wrongdoing was managed based on the student's surname, and students whose parents were troublemakers, it was assumed, followed in those miscreant footsteps. Though my administration could be quite lenient with some students, many times they sought to over-punish students who were the usual suspects. Many of those students ended up especially close to me because I would stand up for them when it was obvious that they had absolutely no part in the issue or that the school was itching for an excuse to expel them when a simple detention or suspension was adequate. Growing up, I was the goody-two-shoes of my graduating class; realizing that I had become the patron teacher of perceived lost causes made me chuckle to myself. In one year, I had undergone a metamorphosis in which I stopped believing that the 'best' students were the ones who were innately talented and always made A's. Rather, my best students were those who came to school and participated in class despite staying up all night with a baby sibling or niece/nephew, working until 11 to help pay bills, or being verbally abused by parents.

By the end of my first year of teaching, I had learned a lot about myself as a person and as an educator. I discovered that my default nervous demeanor is to be stone-faced and serious, but that once I relaxed and allowed my students to see my quirky personality—to actually see Kendra on occasion instead of just Miss McPheeters—it enabled me to have a relationship with them in which I could speak to them as young adults and earn their trust and respect. We could have fun in the classroom and learn at the same time. I proved to myself that my initial assessment that teachers are not only educators but entertainers was correct; when I could come up with silly ways of remembering literary elements or spoke in different 'characters' throughout the lesson, my students stayed more engaged and retained more information. Students began hanging around my room after class, which I took as an opportunity not only to get to know them as people, but to slip in a little extra knowledge about our units as well. My freshmen were still behind; how could they not be when they watched (the same) movies three days a week for years before they had me? I was furious with their prior education, enraged with myself for not being able to catch them up in one year, and disheartened at the prospect of their being behind for the rest of their educational careers. Added to all of these concerns, I knew that my students were only compartmentalizing their prejudiced attitudes. Pejoratives that I would not allow in my classroom were still used in the hallways and outside of school. Looking back on those two years, I was only regulating behaviors in one small sphere of their lives. I made myself into an 'other' again simply "by defining and regulating which knowledge, values, and behavior are considered legitimate and what can be thought or said" without getting to the heart of their cultural influences (Groenke and Nespor, 2010, p. 59). I was slowly coming into my own as a teacher, though. My lessons were easier for me to plan since I knew where my students stood academically. I stopped being Miss McPheeters and became McPheets, a teaching persona whose lessons were effective and rarely forgettable. My students were making progress, though not at the rate I had hoped. Then I was called into my principal's office.

The whole time I had worked at my school, my intent was to only stay one year and then move to Northwest Indiana to be with my husband. Despite my successes at my rural school, I still longed for another suburban school like my student teaching placement in which my only classroom management issue had been proving to my students that I was indeed smart enough to be in the presence of such demigods of academia. Those students were less emotionally taxing since I did not go home worrying about how they would be treated that evening. My current department head was retiring, however, and my principal asked to see me. He told me how wonderful a teacher I was, that they wanted me teaching English full time the next year instead of splitting my time with remediation, and offered me AP English Language and Composition, English 10, developmental reading, and two semester electives of my choice. He finished the conversation with a wink, saying, "Hopefully this means you will quit looking for another job." There was no way I could refuse. I developed the curricula for debate, etymology, and developmental reading over the summer and revised how Advanced Placement would be taught since the school had never achieved a passing score. I threw myself into my work and loved every second of planning, picturing how my students would react to the activities. I went into my second year of teaching nervous about how I would manage the increased grading and planning load as well as how I would tackle two high stakes classes, with AP having the College Board exam and English 10 taking the End of Course Assessment (or ECA, Indiana's graduation qualifying exam), yet confident that I would not only survive but succeed.

In my second year of teaching, I entered my classroom smiling. I only had one room to manage, and for the most part my students were the same group of kids I had taught the year before; in fact, the first semester elective that I had chosen—debate—was overwhelmingly populated by sophomores who took the class solely because they wanted a second class with me. I was both flattered and moved by their desire to spend another hour of the day in my classroom. This year I did not have to plan lessons, classroom expectations, and course descriptions based on conjecture. I walked into my classroom with five binders (one per prep) each containing the course description, syllabus, classroom expectations, plagiarism rules, homework contract, parent letter, and lessons. I was amazed at how in one year I had progressed from sloppy folders in a filing cabinet and staying up until all hours of the night planning lessons just to scrap it the next day for something better, to being a prepared teacher cognizant of her students' needs and developmental levels. By the end of the summer, instead of anxiety, I actually missed my students and looked forward to being back in my own classroom with them.

During the first couple of weeks of the school year, I realized just how easy it was to get back into my routine with my students. My sophomores even commented that my class seemed to start off more smoothly than some of their other classes; when I asked why, they slowly realized that they already knew my expectations and did not have to acclimate to a new setting. This environment was familiar to them. Though some of my policies had changed as I recognized that perhaps a point system for behavior was unnecessary at the high school level—I was new and desperate, having never really dealt with classroom management issues before—and that the 'freebie' I gave once per nine weeks allowing a student to turn in a homework assignment one day late without deduction should not be given to upperclassmen, we smoothly transitioned from a first, chaotic year into one that required minimal reminders as to what was expected in my room.

These first few weeks were also the time period in which I discovered that I did in fact enjoy my job at a small, rural, seemingly backward school. Because we had not met Adequate Yearly Progress (AYP) the year before, we were implementing new practices such as developmental reading in order to remedy our failings. I also loved that my administrators gave me so much freedom to express myself creatively in the classroom and trusted me with such high stakes classes as AP Language and Composition and English 10. My teaching friends were awestruck that a second-year teacher would be gifted with AP, the most coveted of classes with the highest caliber of seniors. The autonomy granted to me also allowed me to teach more controversial themes and topics in AP, as was explicitly stated in the students' parent letter, from reading and discussing elements of Marx's *Communist Manifesto* and applying them to Orwell's *1984* to the low-brow innuendo employed by Chaucer in *The Wife of Bath's Tale* and Shakespeare in *Hamlet*.

Of course, there were still multiple days in which my students' cultural and literary failings both shocked and aggravated me. Though I was analyzing British literature with seniors, their lack of writing instruction meant that they believed anything over a three-page paper to be college-level writing. Their first essay began a battle between a poorly utilized thesaurus and me, culminating in a lesson with seniors about how context is imperative in writing. "You can't use 'equation' when you originally used 'problem' in the sense of there being an issue." My other classes struggled even more. A multi-grade developmental reading class thought the sentence, "i ain't gonna touch that there snake bobby shouted jeff" looked and sounded just fine except for the capitalization errors and a missing period at the end. An entire classroom could not tell me in what years the Civil War was fought—and, in fact, were not even guessing in the right century, having chosen the early twentieth as a good point in time for a civil war—were convinced that there was another part of speech known as the pro-verb, strongly believed that Dickens' *Great Expectations* was written in Elizabethan English, and assumed that the Sahara was a country in Europe somewhere near the Middle East (which apparently also resided in Europe). These moments were cruelly hilarious, and I do cherish being able to take a misconception and help guide students through it. The explanations consumed a few minutes of class time, but my students truly believed these things (by year two, I knew when my students were about to lie to me before they opened their mouths; they weren't very good at it) and I felt compelled to set the record straight before they blurted out these fallacies in a college classroom or with peers in the workforce who knew better.

In the last month of school, I began having panic attacks more frequently than usual. Sophomores were starting to break down because they were so nervous about the End of Course Assessment. They knew they had been behind their entire freshman year and that I had been pushing them even harder this year, citing that we had to do a lot of work for them to catch up to grade-level. While they complained that we had not prepared for the test, I assured them that the past two years with me had taught them the skills that they would need in order to prove that they understood and could apply state standards. The only teaching I did that was in direct preparation for the test was to spend a week honing our timed writing skills before the exam. My AP class was no less stressed. They knew that no student in our school had ever earned a three or higher on the AP Language and Composition exam and were afraid that they would continue that legacy. I told them that the difference between those students and this class was partly the fact that we covered an enormous time span with British literature and did not focus almost solely on Shakespeare, and partly that the new teacher had taken the AP exam herself only six years prior and student taught AP with a school that consistently earned fives, the highest score. I built up my students' confidence in their abilities while simultaneously second-guessing my own. What if my students had not retained the material and I had neglected to notice? I tortured myself with worst-case scenarios in which the vast majority of my students failed due to my horrible teaching and inability to connect lessons to modern day adolescence.

Though I am not a proponent of high-stakes standardized testing—in fact, I am fervently against it—my best day in the classroom was being able to dance from the hallway back into my class and announce to my three sections of English 10 that they had passed the graduation qualifying exam with an 85 percent pass rate, a whopping 23 percent increase from the previous year. I nearly cried. Not only did I work to get my students caught up in a way that did not teach to the test, but we actually met all of the state standards before the test window and had three weeks at the end of the year for a bonus unit analyzing advertisements and propaganda within various media rather than needing to go back over all of the standards that were covered on the exam. On the last day of school I had the distinct pleasure of standing in front of my first students, who had been with me for both years, and telling them for the first time that they were ahead of where they were required to be. I fought back tears and the urge to hug each one of them, though many hugs were had before I left the school for the last time. I finally saw confidence in the faces of my students whose classroom deficiencies had been the result of years of poor teaching and low expectations. Furthermore, I finally saw myself as a true educator—more emotionally invested than the books say I should have been, but an educator who had the opportunity to provide positive change in the lives of her students.

At the conclusion of my two years at my school, I found myself confident and comfortable within the classroom and outside of it. Within two weeks of leaving my first school, I was hired by a much larger rural school in Northwest Indiana as an English teacher and half-time literacy coach, mostly thanks to my work in remediation and my reading endorsement. Instead of panicking before the interviews, I strode in knowing that I am a good teacher who has tested and proven results. (In fact, shortly after my hire date, I learned that three of my seven AP students had passed the exam, with one student earning a four.) My little nest was a wonderful place in which to spend the first two years of my teaching career with a small staff and a community that eventually embraced newcomers, though it was hard to fathom in that first month that it would ever be the case. I believe I was accepted because I strove to understand how my students, their parents, and my coworkers saw their community and the world at large. White and Reid (2008) posit that this desire to understand is essential to being a successful rural teacher and state, "As teachers come to know, and know about, a particular rural place and come to understand its relationships to, and with, other places, they are developing knowledge, sensitivities, awareness, skills, and attitudes that will allow them to feel more at home and powerful in a rural setting" (p. 6). Learning about the community in which I worked helped me tremendously in making material accessible and relevant to my students, in earning the respect and trust of their parents, and in integrating myself into the area. I wish that my university had emphasized that becoming a member of the community outside of school and its extracurricular activities is essential to being a truly effective teacher. In my first two years, I grew with my students, whom I lovingly called my guinea pigs, and was forthright about this being a learning process for all of us.

On my last day, I sat with my students just enjoying one another's company; flashes from the last two years—the good, bad, and funny—passed through my mind. Students and parents thanked me and told me how much they would miss me. I had entered my first school telling myself that it was only a job (a poor attempt at hardening a sensitive personality), and as I packed the last box in my car, took one last glimpse at a room that once again looked like a prison cell, turned in my key, and prepared to drive out of the looking glass for the last time, I realized that my students had made it a home.

References

Groenke, S.L., & Nespor, J. (2010). The drama of their daily lives: Racist language and struggles over the local in a rural high school. In K. A. Schafft and A. Youngblood Jackson (Eds.), *Rural education for the twenty-first century: Identity, place, and community in a globalizing world* (pp. 51–71). University Park, PA: The Pennsylvania University Press.

White, S., & Reid, J. (2008). Placing teachers? Rural schooling through place-consciousness in teacher education. *Journal of Research in Rural Education, 23*(7).

6

IS THERE SUCH A THING AS CARING TOO MUCH? A FARM GIRL SWIMS WITH SHARKS

Chea Parton

SOUTHERN WELLS COMMUNITY SCHOOLS, PONETO, INDIANA

> As in industry, the price of worship at the altar of efficiency is the alienation of the worker from his work—where continuity and wholeness of the enterprise are destroyed for those who engage in it.
>
> (Kliebard, 1975, p. 66)

I thought that because I grew up in a rural community and attended a rural school, I would be best suited for teaching in that same environment; however, I found that teaching in a rural area had many more challenges than I anticipated. Lack of technological resources, lack of funding for various things, frugality to a fault, tractor lust, lack of tolerance for various people groups, and a general disregard for the importance of English in what my students like to call "the real world," coursed through the hallways and invaded my classroom. It was a constant battle against these prevailing hegemonic forces to bring my students to believe that education was worth something. Parents who had always been farmers, factory workers, or habitually unemployed, encouraged their kids, whether aloud or by action, that education was not as important as teachers made it seem. That fact compounded with the natural teenage tendency for apathy was grossly detrimental to the learning environment.

As much as these things frustrated me, the rewards were sweet and ample enough to keep me trying my best, whether or not my students tried theirs. On several occasions I considered giving up and looking at charter schools or graduate school, but just at that moment of doubt, I would receive a note from a student, a parent, or a fellow educator that brought me back from the edge. I became a teacher to make a difference. The challenges of teaching in a rural school obviously made life difficult, but those few moments when I realized that I had succeeded ultimately made teaching in a rural school rewarding.

Throughout all of my practicums and observations, most teachers and teacher educators seemed to agree that the first year of teaching is the most difficult. For me, this was not the case. I was ecstatic to find a job at all (even though it was just two weeks before school was scheduled to start), let alone in the rural area I desired. I had a great mentor, I was given a level of autonomy and freedom in my classroom that I did not expect, and I quickly established myself as a good teacher. When I accepted the job, I was told that there was no set curriculum for any of my classes, which included sophomores, AP Literature, Advanced Composition, and regular seniors. I could essentially mold each course into whatever I wanted. Though I was incredibly intimidated by this, I was thrilled with the freedom and opportunity to be creative with my units. In many of my education courses, we created individual unit plans, but never an entire year's worth of them. To be honest, I had no idea where to start. I spent many days in my classroom sprucing it up in an attempt to make it look less like a room in an asylum and more like the creative learning environment I wanted it to be. I took endless inventories of the novels and books at my disposal in an attempt to come up with some sort of game plan for the year. In retrospect, I think I floundered more than I thought I did, but at the time it was hard to tell. In our entire English department there were only four teachers, and three of us had just been hired with little to no experience. Our department head had only taught for four years, so needless to say, the entire department was a bit green. We helped each other the best we could, and prepared for the year.

The night before the first day of school I could hardly sleep. So many thoughts and anxieties bounced around in my brain. Would I get along with my colleagues? How would the students respond to an outsider? Those questions and a million 'what-do-I-do-ifs' kept me awake for much of that night. Teacher day went smoothly and for the most part, my new colleagues were encouraging and helpful. I did feel a bit out of place being the youngest teacher there, but I decided it might not be so bad. I had a lot to learn and was in a room full of people who could teach me.

A few weeks in, I decided to attempt to teach my sophomore students the complexities of gender issues in *The Awakening*. Before tackling the novel, we discussed gender issues in nineteenth-century America as they compared to today, and we read "The Story of an Hour" to introduce Chopin's writing style as well as the themes with which she was concerned. I was amazed at the fight they put up. My classroom resounded with complaints almost daily: they didn't like it, they couldn't understand it, why didn't she just get divorced, etc. We fought our way through it, and a few creative group activities helped quell their frustration. At the end of the novel, I handed out a list of projects from which they were to choose one creative and one analytical project. I showed them examples of projects that my AP students had done that looked similar. They were really curious to know how to dye paper and make it look old, and seemingly interest was up. Close to the due date, a very grave looking principal approached my room and asked to see me outside. I was terrified. Apparently one of my students had told her parents that she had to write "her suicide note for Miss Parton's class." Just a few days before this, a Norwell student had committed suicide and this parent was concerned that the two were related. Instead of calling me, this parent had called a school board member who was a friend of the family who then called my principal, who then approached my classroom with concern. I was relieved that he was on my side from the start, defending my judgment and competence. Since this incident, I have experienced something similar a few times. In every incident, someone higher up in the food chain was contacted, and in every incident I was defended and supported by my boss. I guess in a community where everyone knows everyone else, being the outsider means that you aren't contacted directly with concerns. However, I respect and appreciate that my principal had enough confidence in my abilities to be on my side before he even heard my version of the story.

For the next unit, I chose to read *Night* with students and discuss the atrocities of the Holocaust. We watched interviews with Elie Wiesel, discussed the novel, and explored hatred between groups of people. My students were interested, invested, and moved by the memoir as well as the history behind it. We made photomontages concerning emotions that affected us the most and built a Holocaust Memory Wall outside of my classroom. We read and wrote mystery stories, which I put in the library for other students to read. We watched the *Power of One* and discussed apartheid in the context of large-scale bullying after which my students created plans to eliminate bullying at Southern Wells. We read *Lord of the Flies* and discussed the danger of living apart from societal rules.

Throughout all of these units, I was appalled by the lack of knowledge, tolerance, and understanding my students had for people different from themselves. I had to remove two students from class for using the n-word, fielded many questions about homosexuality and transexuality, and attempted to gently and honestly correct their misconceptions. Throughout those units and discussions I realized how much of the rural me I had left in Gaston, Indiana, when I attended Purdue University. By disposition, I wasn't afraid of meeting new people or making friends with others who were different from me in any way. Everyone harbors some sort of prejudice, including me, but the diversity that existed at Purdue was refreshing and so much more interesting than homogenous, 99.9 percent white, Wes-Del High School ever was. The university changed me more than I realized, and I was quickly finding that those changes made me liberal in the eyes of Southern Wells and the surrounding community.

In many ways, I felt subversive for attempting to have honest conversations with kids who were so misinformed and intolerant, yet eager to discuss taboo topics. I joked with my family that I'd been called down to the principal's office more as a teacher than I ever was as a student. While this is true, I think it's important to teach young people about tolerance, kindness, and that there's already enough hate in the world. There's no need for them to add to it. Because teenagers are by default myopic, it was perhaps a losing battle, but I kept telling myself, "At least I'm fighting."

For the most part, parents and students were receptive to me, my creativity, and my push for students to think. The only problems I had that first year seemed to be with the senior boys in my general English class. One in particular enjoyed challenging me and my underdeveloped classroom management skills. It was a relief when he transferred out of my class to take another in order to graduate early. I realized that it wouldn't always be so easy to avoid such confrontations, but I was glad that this time was so easy. It definitely wouldn't be in future situations, but at that time, my optimism was high. I still believed in the power of education and my ability to reach students. I received several e-mails from parents thanking me for my work with their students. Many highlighted my influence on their child's confidence level and knowledge in my subject area. I even had a student who seemed to be constantly in trouble for skipping his study hall to attend one of my higher level classes. No one in the office believed me when I told them. I seemed to have a knack for reaching the 'bad' kids. Those students that other teachers complained about in the lounge. The students with bad attitudes and poor work ethics. These accolades continued to fuel my optimism. The students, though they maintained that they still didn't like English, admitted that they loved my class. They were relating to me as a person, perhaps because I treated them like people as well. After my guest appearance at the talent contest, 'Raider Idol,' you would have thought that I was a genuine celebrity. It felt good to be a teacher. Despite the small paycheck and long hours, I loved my job and was excited to go to work every day.

The year ended with a positive review from my principal and a few of those nice e-mails, but it also ended after only 62 percent of my sophomore students passed the state standardized test. I had never been a D student, and I was not about to be a D teacher. I was told that this was a common trend, but for me it was disappointing and discouraging. If I was doing the amazing work with students that everyone seemed to think I was doing, why were their scores so low? It seemed that maybe I focused too much on helping students use their imaginations and not enough on the 'skill and drill' questioning strategies used on the End of Course Assessment (ECA) administered by the state. The more I thought about it, the more disgruntled I became. I reflected back on the review work I did with my students. I thought about the conferences I went to and the overwhelming lack of resources to help students prepare. The website contained only one practice test, so I ended up using an old ISTEP manual I found. How do they expect us to perform well if they don't give us adequate resources to prepare? I didn't want to compromise my belief in creative thinking; nor did I want to deprive my students of the ability to think outside the box. But a brief reality check told me that the scores had to be better. I resolved to do my best to blend my current methods with the skill and drill methods that would help my students be more successful on that standardized test.

At the end of the year, we were informed that we would be transitioning from a block schedule to seven 50-minute periods. This didn't bother me as much as it did many of the other teachers who were set in their ways. Many of the other faculty members complained about it, but I was hoping that it would help my students have English year round instead of every other block. I searched for methods books to help me. I read a couple books, Lemov's (2010) *Teach Like a Champion* and Copeland's (2005) *Socratic Circles: Fostering Critical and Creative Thinking in Middle and High School*, during the summer that I hoped would help alter my perspective on testing as well as my attitude about being forced to bow to it. In some ways they were helpful, but in others I vehemently disagreed with them. I tried to find more resources to help my students practice their ECA skills, but found nothing, especially nothing free. I was frustrated, and that is not how I wanted to begin my second year. It seemed that even from the beginning of year two my bubble of optimism had burst, and I was starting the year closer to the kind of teacher I never wanted to be. I promised myself that I would never let the system break me. That I would never become the teacher who made learning altogether tedious, taking my frustrations out on my students. I started year two off on the wrong foot, and though there were times I seemed to be on the right one, the year was trying and tasking.

Teacher day arrived, and once again, I found it difficult to sleep. Instead of anxiety, dread kept me up that night. I awoke in the morning attempting to have a good attitude, but I drove all 35 miles wanting to turn around. In our staff meeting that morning, we discussed the abysmal nature of our pass rate on the English ECA, and I felt every eye bore into me like it was somehow my fault because I have every single sophomore in the building. It was a surreal moment because somehow I managed to feel guilty about their scores as well as outraged that everyone in the room seemed to agree that it was my fault. What about the teachers before me who taught the same students? What about all of the content area teachers who possess the capability to help students with their literacy but choose not to? Behind me I heard the principal ask, "Who here thinks that this was all this young lady's responsibility?" No one answered him, but I knew they were all thinking it. He went on to say, "We all have a hand in this. We're a team, and we all need to step it up." It was good that he didn't blame me, but I found it hard to believe that no one else in the faculty blamed me, especially because I found it so easy to blame myself.

It seemed that the universe heard my plea for more resources because I was delivered a copy of a practice manual and practice tests that day. After meeting with the rest of the English department and the principal, we decided that, like another school in the area, we would implement a common assessment system where we would deliver similar assessments across the freshman and sophomore classes every four and a half weeks and use data collected from them to determine our mastery levels of each of the skills/standards on the ECA tests. After which, we would reteach the skills that were lacking. It took some doing and quite a bit of extra work, but I was optimistic that this would help our scores, and I didn't feel so alone in the effort anymore.

Along with this new system, in order to improve our analytical reading capabilities and interpersonal skills, I implemented Socratic circles. I chose every genre, including songs, connecting to each of the units to attempt to engage students. I was impressed by most of the students' efforts to be prepared, annotate well, think deeply, and talk with one another. So far, so good. Except that I was stretched thin, getting less sleep than last year, and battling a completely new group of students. I don't know if some of my novelty wore off, or this group was particularly rebellious, but they tried me much more, and without my bubble of optimism, pushed me until I broke down in front of them. It was the perfect storm. I was working so hard, the compliments had grown scarcer, more was being asked of me, and I felt underappreciated by faculty, administration, and students alike. I was broken.

I think the downward spiral started the day we discussed student literacy in the professional development meeting we had before school. I think it was the principal attempting to remind the faculty that we were all responsible for helping our kids be better readers, not just the English department. The group of colleagues with whom I was sitting seemed supportive and glad to have the strategies we discussed. Not everyone agreed though. One faculty member in particular, I call her Negative Nancy, complained to me after the meeting. It wasn't her job; English wasn't her subject, she doesn't have enough time to squeeze it into her curriculum, and they've been pushing literacy for 15 years and she was sick of hearing about it. Inside I was boiling. I turned to her and very calmly told her that the fact that they'd been talking about it for 15 years was probably because it wasn't getting any better, and maybe, just maybe, if she made an effort to implement some of the strategies here and there it would get better and we wouldn't have to listen to it for the next 15 years. I also told her that I noticed that the one area of the state exam where her students proved most inadequate relied most heavily on interpreting written language. After this little altercation, I walked back into my classroom in an attempt to calm down before my students arrived.

After that incident, I felt alone again like one soldier fighting an entire army of students and state legislators. Making my $6.39 per hour on 75-hour workweeks, I continued to fight. With little energy and less optimism, I tried to do right by my students. I threw all I had into every lesson, attempting to make each lesson as beneficial and engaging as possible, only to be met with complaints about them constantly. My biggest complainers, I'll call them Josh and Jonathon, had the worst case of tractor lust I've ever seen. My class was a joke to them because they didn't need English to be a farmer. All they needed was a working tractor and daylight. They had no idea what it takes to run a farming business. I grew up on a pretty small farm managed by parents who were raised by farmers, but I knew enough to realize that you need more than a tractor, truck, and sunshine. According to them, though, I still knew nothing about it. I tried to reach them with tough love, documentation and research, and humor, but nothing worked. My class and its attempt to improve their lives was just another part of their day they had to endure before they could go home, hop on the tractor, and get into the fields. For the most part I endured. I tried to remind myself that they were teenagers who were predisposed to think they knew everything when really they knew nothing. I tried to empathize and understand their position, but there came the day when I just couldn't.

I was trying to discuss *Lord of the Flies* with them, fielding the class's questions, and attempting to connect the questions we were answering to the types of questions they would see on the ECA. I was exhausted, it was fifth period, my second to last period of the day, and I was ready to go home. I was fielding a question from a student, and formulating a response. I spoke the words "I don't," then paused to think carefully about the wording of the response. I then heard Joshua finish my sentence with "teach." I tried with what little energy and strength I had left to hold back my tears until the bell rang, but I couldn't do it. I told them to get started on their homework and turned to my computer screen, sobbing.

I tried to pull it together for my sixth period class, but I'm sure I looked like I'd been hit by a train. The Advanced Composition students entered my class as raucous as usual, until they saw me, that is. They were all concerned; I assured them that I was okay, and did my best to make it through their lesson. I managed to do okay until seventh period was finally there. It was my prep and I spent most of it crying. I needed to talk to someone, so I headed to the library to talk to another one of the English teachers who I knew was supervising a study hall that hour. I needed so badly to hear that he wasn't right. That I was a good teacher. She couldn't leave the study hall, so I broke down in front of a group of 15 or so students. I didn't know what to do. I wondered aloud if I should seek employment at a charter or magnet school designed for people who intrinsically appreciated their education. I know it was not the time nor place, but I didn't know what else to do, so I melted down in front of everyone.

In retrospect, I know this wasn't the right thing to do, and it seems a bit dramatic, but at the time, I felt completely defeated and like I had nowhere to turn. As serendipity would have it, the principal walked into the library in the midst of my breakdown. We talked about the situation, he was encouraging, but I don't think he really knew what to do with me. On my way out of the library, the librarian handed me a note written anonymously by a student and addressed to me. She wouldn't tell me who it was, but she did tell me it would probably surprise me. I waited until I returned to my room to open and read it. It made me cry even harder, but in a good way. The following is an excerpt:

> I want to apologize for people's actions toward you. Kids in high school are like sharks in a shark tank and they do not care about your feelings. So don't take what they do or say personally. You are a great person you care about kids who do not understand what you do to help them. But if you keep up the work people will appreciate what you do. You are a rarity to people today, you have a dream and you don't want to stop until it's realized. I respect that and it should be respected but so many people are so overcome with themselves now a days they can not see how hard other people try. . . . Just

remember no matter how hard things may get you can never give up on your dreams never give up what you are passionate about, because once you do that what is life worth? . . . They might not know it but the fundamentals you teach them every day with your showing of understanding your persistence to care will come to them one day when they are in a dark place. . . . Well I hope this brings you up it saddens me to have seen you like this. You may not know who wrote this but just know there are people who care about how hard you try . . .

I never found out who wrote this, but it completely changed the way I felt about my job. Even rereading it, I'm inspired to have a better attitude. Despite the fact that it is riddled with grammatical errors, the sincerity of the note and genuine appreciation for what I do was so touching. I decided that maybe Southern Wells was the place for me after all. I came to school the next day ready to go. At least until my fifth period class. I was still finding it hard to be encouraged in the face of a class of 30 sophomores who couldn't possibly care any less about the ECA or their futures as productive citizens. I battled it out managing to maintain composure in the face of frustration, received an apology from the student who boldly declared that I don't teach, and marched on toward the ECA.

Even though I was frustrated and struggling, it seemed that there were just enough encouraging moments to balance everything out. Another one of these moments was at 'Raider Idol.' Because there are so few teachers at Southern Wells, we all chip in when it comes to extracurriculars. I played guitar and sang for my classes, especially when we began poetry, so I was a standing guest performer at the spring talent contest, Raider Idol. Another faculty member had expressed interest in performing a duet with me, we'd tried to make time to practice, but we were both busy and it was difficult. As a result, we weren't as good as either of us thought we should be, but the night of the show we were there and as ready as we would ever be. As soon as they announced my name, the crowd went wild. There was screaming, vigorous clapping, and whistling. I felt like the fifth Beatle, and it felt good. We performed our song; it went all right, and the clapping, screaming, and whistling once again ensued. When we got off stage, my duet partner turned to me and said something I'll never forget: "Listen to that." (They were still applauding.) "Don't ever try to tell me that you aren't making a difference for these kids." It struck me like a slap in the face. It was a wake-up call. She was right.

More weeks of reading, writing, and ECA preparation went by, and I was growing very nervous. A couple of other staff members and I performed a skit that I wrote about good test-taking practices. The kids thought it was hilarious and claimed they enjoyed it. I just hoped they would remember to eat a good breakfast and get plenty of sleep like the skit demonstrated. Testing week came, and from what they told me, my students felt fairly confident that they were doing well, and I hoped they were right. We forged on into *The Power of One* and the bullying depicted in the film, the book, and other short stories as I waited for our results with trepidation.

Because they took the state exam, I decided to give them a final project instead of a final exam. We were working on them when the scores came in. The principal walked in with a grave look on his face, so I was worried. He asked if it was okay to invade my personal bubble. Confused, I told him that was fine. He gave me a hug and told me that our English ECA scores came in. Our pass rate was 80 percent. I almost cried. Last year's pass rate was 62 percent. I know I'm only an English teacher, but even I know 18 percent is a substantial increase. I couldn't believe it! On the one hand, I was ecstatic that we improved, but on the other hand I was disappointed that it had to matter so much. In the following days, I received many accolades and congratulations from my colleagues, which helped to keep me fueled for the sprint that was the end of the year. Graduation brought many teary-eyed thank-yous from seniors, even e-mails from them as they began summer classes, thanking me for certain activities or lessons that we completed. I decided it was a good year.

Sitting down to do an overhaul on my course syllabi, certain units, and course organization, I realized that next year the bar sits quite a bit higher than last. Right now I feel up to the challenge, but who knows what the school year will bring. Even looking back on these last two years as I write this, I think of a student who once said to me, "Miss P., you know what your problem is? You care too much." I wonder, do I? Is there such a thing as caring too much? My colleagues maintain that in time I'll develop a thick skin and their comments won't get to me as much, but I'm not convinced as I look at some of their relationships with students that this is a good thing. None of my methods classes covered preparing students for standardized tests or caring too much or wanting more for students than they want for themselves or not becoming a defeated wreck in front of students. Maybe if they had, I'd be a better teacher. For now, I've decided that I can only be me. Me with all of my faults and flaws. Me with my passions and frustrations. Me the farm girl who went to Purdue not for agriculture but education. For now, I guess that must be good enough.

Recently, I read an article, "Good Teaching in Difficult Times: Demoralization in the Pursuit of Good Work," published by Doris Santoro in the *American Journal of Education*. It reminded me of some of my colleagues' warnings against burnout. I remember thinking, this is only my second year; how could I possibly be burning out? Santoro (2011) describes what I experienced not in terms of burnout but demoralization. Because my situation was one in which I began to ask myself if what I was doing mattered, if it was "bettering the world or myself," she asserts that I have fallen prey not to burnout but demoralization (p. 2). She argues that the ethical value of what teachers do is enough to sustain their work despite the lack of monetary or material reward. When that moral reward is taken away, when teachers are forced to teach to the test, when their units are no longer structured around higher level and critical thinking, when state-mandated high-stakes testing replaces the journey of learning, teachers like me become demoralized and we question if what we're doing is indeed teaching, let alone worthwhile.

Throughout my entire first two years, and even now, I find that I frequently ask myself if I'm a good teacher. I never know through which lens to look when answering this question—my own or the state's. Santoro distinguishes between good teaching and successful teaching, asserting that "one could be a wildly successful teacher and enjoy none of the moral rewards of teaching. The current policy environment has privileged successful teaching to such a degree that the goals of current initiatives may eclipse the possibility for good teaching" (p. 9). So now the question becomes, do I want to be a good teacher or a successful teacher? Do I want to be successful in the state's game or my own? Do I sacrifice my own educational philosophy for theirs even though I feel in every atom of my being that it's wrong? Or do I continue to try to blend the two, surviving on little sleep, missed meals, and no personal life? I don't know that I've completely reached a verdict on this, and frankly, I'm still more than a little incensed that I even have to ask myself those questions.

I was one teacher in one classroom. I was responsible for roughly 125 students. And with little resources to overcome what seemed to be an overwhelming amount of teenage sloth and myopia as well as tractor lust, I was responsible for achieving a successful pass rate on the ECA for my 84 sophomores. But I was also one teacher in one classroom responsible to herself, her philosophies, and what she defined as learning. In those conflicting subjectivities, it was difficult to form a whole and concise identity as Miss Parton, rural English teacher. I was experiencing what Alsup (2004) called a "fundamental paradox" (p. 37), trying to balance who I was and who the school and culture at large expected me to be. I was indeed on a "seemingly impossible seesaw to balance" (p. 37). But, maybe along the way they'll come together a little more readily. I suppose I'll just have to take the sage advice from my anonymous student to keep striving to realize my dreams and keep swimming with those sharks.

References

Alsup, J. (2004). Am I a teacher? Exploring the development of professional identity. *Language Arts Journal of Michigan*, 20(1), 35–39.

Copeland, M. (2005). *Socratic circles: Fostering critical and creative thinking in middle and high school*. Portland, ME: Stenhouse Publishers.

Kliebard, H.M. (1975). Bureaucracy and curriculum theory. In W.F. Pinar (Ed.), *Curriculum theorizing: The reconceptualists* (pp. 51–69). Berkeley, CA: McCutchan Publishing.

Lemov, D. (2010). *Teach like a champion: 49 techniques that put students on the path to college*. San Francisco, CA: Jossey-Bass Inc. Pub.

Santoro, D. (2011). Good teaching in difficult times: Demoralization in the pursuit of good work. *American Journal of Education*, 118(1), 1–23.

PART II

Teaching Through Place: Mid- to Late-Career Teacher Narratives

7

TEACHING THROUGH PLACE: MID- TO LATE-CAREER TEACHER NARRATIVES

Lisa Schade Eckert and Janet Alsup

The experienced teachers in the following chapters tell of their personal and pedagogical growth and how they came to know themselves both as professionals and community members. Like the early career teachers in the first section, they learned from early mistakes and difficulties; these experiences became gateways on a path leading to expanded breadth and depth of pedagogical knowledge. Significantly, the communities in which they teach are central characters in each narrative, shaping their teaching identities as each of the authors stepped into roles of leadership in their schools and communities, developing relationships within the social spaces that surround their schools and classrooms. Interestingly, the narratives in this section 'speak' to the narratives in the previous section; the experiences narrated in the following pages further develop some of the themes raised by the early career teachers as well as introducing new ones. In essence, and serendipitously, the experienced teachers respond to their less experienced colleagues. The experiences these mid- to late-career teachers narrate reveal much about the advantages and challenges inherent in many teaching environments, but they also provide a glimpse into the ways in which teaching in a rural community can become a career-long love affair with a unique place and the people who live there.

Emerging Themes in the Mid- to Late-Career Narratives
Policy and Professional Development

This is an important theme extended from the first section but, in significant contrast, *none* of the experienced teachers emphasized the importance of standardization or testing in writing about his or her experiences as a rural teacher. We find this incredibly important in understanding the reasons why a teacher stays in education, and why a rural teacher in particular stays in the same school community. The teachers in this section have largely transcended the boundaries imposed by an emphasis on test results; to them, testing is a reality but does not define who they are as educators or overly prescribe curricular design. Whether this is because they have been teaching for a long time and their pedagogical development predates the current emphasis on testing, or because they have more autonomy in their rural teaching situations (as they will describe in their chapters), is difficult to conclude from the narrative data; the bottom line is that none of these teachers found their muse in the bubbles of a test answer sheet or margins of a preparation guide. Instead, they found inspiration from professional development experiences and immersion in the school community. We speculate that the necessary collaboration of all parties involved in the project of educating children in small communities (teachers, administrators, coaches, parents, and community members) means the tasks inherent in meeting state and federal standards is a group effort. This is not to say such collaboration does not happen in suburban or urban school environments, but when one teacher is responsible for teaching several levels of English, coaching the volleyball team, serving on the school improvement team, and is also the union negotiator and/or fills in as administrator as necessary, that teacher is part of a unique team of educators who each do a little of everything and, consequently, share the responsibilities for measuring school success.

It is impossible to overemphasize the importance of quality, sustained, and rigorous professional development for teachers. This can come in many forms: graduate classes, summer institutes on university campuses, initiatives created by private entities designed to facilitate understanding and/or compliance with state/federal mandates (e.g., the Common Core State Standards). The requirements for teacher professional development and continued licensure vary by state, but virtually all public K-12 teachers are required to pursue professional development opportunities to maintain licensure. The narratives in this section represent what professional development can (and should) really mean for teacher pedagogical development—it happens with immersion in a sustained and rigorous program that clearly links to teacher practice in local context (Eckert and Alsup, 2010). For example, Hali Kirby-Ertel and Kari Patterson, both teachers in rural Montana schools, participated in the Montana Heritage Project, a professional development opportunity for teachers in Montana focusing on local community history and developing pedagogical goals to closely examine the unique characteristics and events of the locality. Sharon Bishop and Jeffrey Ross found the closest university-based National Writing Project sites and participated in Invitational Summer Institutes. Unfortunately, both of these programs have lost state and federal funding in recent years; we hope that, by highlighting these stories, we can help to provide some rationale for reinstating them. Jeffrey was also selected as a Fellow for the "Teaching Shakespeare through Performance" residency at Shakespeare's Globe in London in 2013, one of 21 teachers from around the United States. Gregg Rutter, Roger Nieboer, Govinda Budrow, and Bambi O'Hern work with university researchers in gifted and talented programs, dismantling stereotypes of struggling Native American rural schools. A key reason experienced rural teachers stay in the profession and in rural schools is reflected in these narratives: Rural teachers often take responsibility for their own professional development and seek quality professional development opportunities beyond those required by individual school districts. As another rural teacher put it, "Whatever catches my attention, I do."

The Role of Language and Discourse of Place

Connecting language and discourse to place is another theme common to the narratives in this section. Experienced teachers adapt to cultural markers and language, or what Burton, Brown, and Johnson (2013) call "the distinctive informal culture found in many rural schools" (p. 5), assimilating them into their pedagogical repertoire; conversely, they adapt their instructional strategies to celebrate and recognize unique elements and events of the local community into shared classroom dialogue. Each of the experienced teachers share stories of learning to focus on local history and the unique nature of the community in which they teach. Sharon highlights local authors and how she incorporated their work in her classroom to use the language of place as a central theme in her curriculum. Hali discovered that the language of hunting and conservation was a flash point for her students and quickly learned to use this language in her ELA instructional plan—she found that students were engaged and immersed in projects examining the role of hunting and conservation in her rural Montana community. Jeffrey describes how cowboy poetry proved to be an entry point into examining poetic language and critical analysis/writing of poetry. Kari employed the local dialect and ranching interests (horses in particular) to engage students in inquiry projects, paying special attention to honoring the local traditions and funds of knowledge as she developed curricula and found the boundaries between her personal rural life and those of her students.

Resilience and Connection with Community

A related theme centers on ways in which teachers demonstrate resiliency as they adapt to the subtle (and not-so-subtle) relationships surrounding the school and community. The teachers in this section describe the difficult process of developing an understanding of the power of their suggestions, discussions, and insights on their students' lives. The unique and public role of a rural teacher often means a teacher must develop a thick skin, yet still remain sensitive to the sensibilities of young people learning about concepts that may be far removed from their community and familial experiences. This requires a certain resilient flexibility, a difficult balance of outsider and insider knowledge, which rural teachers must nurture. Hali, Kari, and Sharon tell of learning when to let students make their own decisions in fulfilling curricular expectations, about having faith in students to learn through place-based inquiry projects inspired by local history and current events. While this is a quality of all good teachers, the role of the community, as well as the role of the teacher in the community, is central to teaching and learning in a rural school.

One unique aspect of teaching in a small community is the extent to which teachers are immersed in their students' lives. The experiences narrated by the teachers in this section detail the deep connection they have with students throughout their schooling—connections forged in several levels of classroom instruction, in extracurricular activities, in community organizations and events, and through extensive knowledge of parents and families. Sherman and Sage (2011) note "the day-to-day interactions between students and teachers were also part of the process of sustaining the [rural] community" and describe "the importance of local teachers as the keepers of the community's social history" (p. 5). "The school system appeared to be a personification of the community itself for many, and an embodiment of its successes and failures . . . often the greatest resource for those in need" (p. 6).

The teacher narratives demonstrate how each of them have stepped into the role of community leader and public intellectual. For example, Gregg, Govinda, Bambi, and Roger have adjusted their understanding of time and methods of curricular planning to become flexibly responsive to their community's rhythms and needs. They understand the unique challenges their students face and respond with love and concern. Kari describes how she learned to balance her personal and public lives, telling a compelling story of love and how that love for students has ideological and emotional boundaries, noting the depth of her grief at the graduation of her first class of students; she learned how to compartmentalize her passion for her teaching and her responsibilities to the families of her students. Hali describes an essay project that led to more than she had anticipated, blurring the lines between school and community. Jeffrey's expectations for a community arts program became a learning experience for him as much as for his students. Interesting in all of these contexts is how present the parents and communities are in the teachers' pedagogical and curricular goals.

Creativity and Imagination

The narratives in this section demonstrate how experienced teachers creatively use available resources; instead of emphasizing what they lack, they describe how they use the unique resources available in their communities. As we mentioned earlier, these lessons and projects go far beyond the requirements of standards, demonstrating creativity and imagination at every level of instructional design. The teachers also tell of their significant role in academic and administrative decision making—they serve in school governance in many capacities, just as they serve in many school extracurricular activities. They describe a level of autonomy that allows them to be creative in curricular design and the ways in which they responded. Jeffrey's talents as a poet and scholar infuse his classes and his community work with creative opportunities for sharing ideas and projects. Poetic language is embedded in Gregg, Govinda, Bambi, and Roger's chapter, illustrating their innovation and joy in developing instructional plans to celebrate the language and stories of their Ojibwe community.

The teachers in this section have been teaching in a rural school long enough to have integrated into their school communities, have learned some tough lessons about being a teacher in unique places, and have successfully taken advantage of the curricular freedom that comes with being the only, or one of two, English teachers in a school. These teachers point to a transformational moment, one that was difficult, when they had to interrogate their ideology and pedagogy, and contemplate what was really important to them as teachers, as learners, and people. And they rose to the task—re-envisioning what the professional and personal task of education was about, and stepping into the role of public intellectual, community organizer, and pedagogical leader.

References

Burton, M., Brown, K., & Johnson, A. (2013). Storylines about rural teachers in the United States: A narrative analysis of the literature. *Journal of Research in Rural Education*, 28(12), 1–18.

Eckert, L. S., & Alsup, J. (2010). Continuing education and the English teacher: How graduate programs transform secondary classrooms. In I. M. Saleh & M. S. Khine (Eds.), *Teaching teachers: Approaches in improving quality of education* (pp. 215–226). New York, NY: Nova Science Publishers.

Sherman, J., & Sage, R. (2011). Sending off all your good treasures: Rural schools, brain-drain, and community survival in the wake of economic collapse. *Journal of Research in Rural Education*, 26(11). Retrieved June 28, 2014, from http://jrre.psu.edu/articles/26–11.pdf.

8

LESSONS FROM THE INSIDE OUT

Poetry, Epiphanies, and Creative Literary Culture in a Rural Montana High School

Jeffrey B. Ross

BELT HIGH SCHOOL, BELT, MONTANA

As a new English teacher at a rural Montana high school, I was confronted with the typical challenges a teacher faces adjusting to a new cultural and educational environment. I worried about my inexperience, the breadth and preparation required for teaching English in grades 9–12 at Belt High School, and my outsider status in the classroom and the community. But countering those concerns was a confidence anchored in my writing and academic experience, having earned an A.B. in English from UC-Davis, and an MFA in poetry from the University of Montana.

Named for the conspicuous 'belt' of sandstone circling nearby Belt Butte, Belt (pop. 600) lies in the bottom of a shallow canyon in Montana's semiarid high plains. A coal mining town at the turn of the twentieth century, Belt contains a mix of ranching, military, and commuting families (Great Falls), and is dominated by Belt Public Schools, a K-12 school with a total enrollment of 300 students, 95 of whom are in high school.

As part of my pedagogical and personal adjustment into the Belt High School community, I established a monthly public prose and poetry reading on the second Tuesday of the month named 'Belt it Out.' Designed for high school students and the local community, this public venue would offer writers an 'authentic audience,' an element important for providing increased focus, relevance, and for my students, independence from the classroom. The readings began in the fall of 2009 at The Belt Theater (c. 1916), a local historical landmark that seems to be perpetually under restoration. I began with the hope of establishing an accessible, welcoming, and popular literary tradition for the school and community. However, the readings only averaged 3–4 participants, mostly students, and by the spring of 2010 I recognized that establishing a monthly reading in Belt would require more than simple promotion and the opportunity to read outside the classroom. On the surface the question appeared straightforward: How could I generate student and public interest in the readings? But the real question, one that I had yet to fully comprehend, was how does a university-trained poet and teacher begin to understand the importance of a genre not only within a community, but also within his own poetic aesthetic? I would learn that any 'transformation' of the Belt community would require a corresponding 'transformation' of my identity as a teacher and writer, from the 'inside out.'

A school's literary culture is more directly a function of all aspects of community, and perhaps it is an obvious point that one cannot decouple the demographics, interests, and experience of community with that of the individual student. George Hillocks (1995) writes, "The environment of the broader culture and its institutions supplies many of the basic tools of writing, tools that . . . lie outside the writer's conscious control" (p. 85). Accordingly, the most obvious extracurricular impediment to the readings appeared to be the ubiquitous sports culture in the school and community. I suspected the dominance of sports left little time or energy for students or the public for nonathletic activities. Many students were clearly focused on athletics, but healthy participation in theater, music, DECA, and FFA demonstrated interest in the arts and other extracurriculars, even if literary performance was a niche 'less witnessed.' Moreover, the school administration supported the readings, and there was no resistance from the community, just a quiet apathy. As a teacher moving into a rural locale, I understood the importance of getting to know my students *and* local community, but clearly the lack of interest with 'Belt it Out' contained lessons I had yet to understand.

In search of public reading models to emulate, I found articles celebrating the success of poetry in the classroom, where it appeared rivers of poetic enthusiasm were flowing in both urban and rural high schools. Tamara Van Wyhe echoed my desires for my students. Using poetry as a daily foundational genre in her classroom, she "saw her tiny rural school become a community of poets" (Van Wyhe, 2006, p. 16). In "'Who Makes Much of a Miracle?' The Evolution of a School's Poetic Culture," Ian Strever (2006) writes of the promise of a teacher succeeding to "reviv[e] his school's poetry elective, and stimulate poetic discussion and creation across [school] departments and the community" (p. 66). So teachers were demonstrating success promoting poetry across the classroom and community.

It was clear that there were a rich variety of models available in the literature, but what about local resources that were perhaps a better cultural fit for Belt? As a new teacher in an unfamiliar rural community, I initially relied almost exclusively on the literature rather than reaching out and establishing personal contacts with teachers in adjacent districts. In retrospect this was an obvious omission. However, at the time I had not yet developed an appreciation for the importance of the 'local' for sources and advice. Nor did I find suitable models locally. Furthermore, even with the ease of the Internet, I was reluctant to approach relative strangers by e-mail with a complex project at the height of the busy school year. In establishing professional relationships, I would find face-to-face contact with colleagues to be essential, a reality contrary to the idea that electronic communication can always adequately mitigate a rural teacher's professional isolation.

In the literature I also found excitement about poetic pedagogy in the classroom and in the broader community from proponents of 'performance poetry,' a sometimes-dramatic oral recitation delivered for an audience. In "Out Loud: The Common Language of Poetry," Ellis, Gere, and Lamberton (2003) begin by positing Robert Scholes' contention that poetry as a taught genre has suffered under the New Critical lens, where poetic theory is favored over poetic experience (p. 44). In other words, poetic pleasure has been subsumed under a pedagogical avalanche of "tone, irony, paradox, and theme," and other clattering literary detritus (p. 44). The argument is to increase the emphasis on oral interpretation, analysis based on emotional connections, rather than analytical interpretation (p. 44). The authors witnessed a level of enthusiasm with 'slam' performance, a competitive reading that rivaled enthusiasm one might find "at a varsity game" (p. 45). For Belt, however, the sports analogy was misplaced; the local support for athletics creates a powerful extrinsic motivation for students and would unlikely transfer to literary performance without a substantial infusion of community involvement. Moreover, I am suspicious of competitive models for a practice that can be highly personal and idiosyncratic. But performance is not always competitive; for some it is the most expressive form, poetry with a robust physicality. Nevertheless, is this athletic model where exteriority is given priority over meaning and the nuances of ambiguity, eliminating the silences and voids that allow a reader/listener entry into a work?

In *Poetry as Survival*, Gregory Orr (2002) writes that "in the personal lyric, the self encounters its existential crises in symbolic form, and the poem that results is a model of this encounter" (p. 22). An excellent example of this 'symbolism' modeling extremis is evident in a poem from Jonathan (a pseudonym), a former Belt senior. Jonathan dropped out of school mid-year, but a few of his poems vividly broke through his academic malaise, an attitude not uncommon, especially with boys in the high school. In "Of Patience" he writes:

I am from a life of darkness,
With stars for guidance,
A horn for reminders,
I am from beautiful running machines,
With rust telling me what is mine,
From the grass growing through the frames,
From the gravel shooting up as they drive,
The reward of patience on an old car,
What a beautiful reminder
Of all the years,
Of patience.

Jonathan's challenges proved too difficult for him to realize his academic potential at Belt. What is remarkable, however, is his gift of metaphor and his ability to write a poem that effortlessly gets to the heart of the matter. His assignment was to write a poem about a car (his main interest), and the only requirement was to use anaphora (repetition) to provide rhythm. This was his creative frame, and in ten minutes he had handwritten "Of Patience," without revision.

Much of Jonathan's personal story is metaphorically apparent in his text, the specifics not necessary to the reader. The voids, the margins, what is unsaid, contain his personal tragedy. I interpret the "beautiful running machines" as an example of T.S. Eliot's *objective correlative*, where Jonathan demonstrates emotions with perceivable objects rather than a direct description; he shows rather than tells us. Here Jonathan speaks through objects he can understand and control. Orr (2002) writes that in poetry "disorder is dynamic" (p. 23), and here Jonathan demonstrates a processing of organic disorder that is unpremeditated, and exposed from the inside out. Is Jonathan's poem a creative accident dependent on the reader to fill those gaps in his "frame," to give it meaning? Perhaps. But if unintended, much of poetry must be as accidental and no less valuable or beautiful to both writer and reader.

There is truth to Orr's argument that "we are creatures whose volatile inner lives are both mysterious to us and beyond our control" (p. 4). He asks the question of how we cope with "the strangeness and unpredictability of our own emotional being?" (p. 4) His answer includes the efficacy of "the personal lyric, the 'I' poem dramatizing inner and outer experience." It is this challenge, this "dramatization" of expression that ultimately draws me to writing, and it does not privilege product over process. If a student can attain a certain 'physicality' with a text, then even the most reluctant writer can become personally engaged and can experience intrinsic motivation for writing, for self-expression. And although teaching is a very complex enterprise, this is the foundation of my approach, to teach English from the perspective of a writer, from the inside out, in a community of student writers.

Nonetheless, as much as I value creative self-expression, I believe in the utility of writing, the necessity of effective and skillful use of language, the power of the essay (and yes, the poem) as an engine for critical thinking, the importance of audience, clarity, and precision. But none of these attributes as projected both pedagogically and as a mode for personal and communal expression were translating into enthusiasm for our public reading, for 'Belt it Out.'

University trained in an MFA setting, my bias leans toward the personal lyric, and although I write and appreciate the sound of formal poetry, my preferences are found in an understated musicality. End rhyme as the controlling mechanism in a poem lacked sophistication in my mind. But what good teacher would negate, limit the scope of any writing style if it suited the author? That is antithetical to the project of *creative* writing. Self-expression has to be a celebration of each individual's voice, regardless of style. Gerald Reyes (2006) writes:

> It is through their own [student] voices where they discover that they have at least one thing in common; that they all have something to say. The voice is exactly what spoken word poetry summons. If we do not honor and encourage what our students have to say and all the experiences that their thoughts have been rooted into, then we limit their whole being.
>
> (p. 10)

But I was beginning to sense a bias against particular forms of poetry, those forms of poetic expression that are public, performative, and perhaps most ironic, popular. I began to question whether I was an elitist.

According to Dana Gioia (2004), skepticism of performance poetry, a genre that includes 'slam,' 'hip-hop,' 'rap,' and 'cowboy' poetry, can appear elitist because "the communities in which [those] genres dwell are far from the 'literati' establishment, such as university MFA programs" (p. 12). This elitism can be manifest regardless of the fact that the oral tradition has roots deeper than any written word. Moreover, the rhythms they incorporate, the rhyme and meter, are more formal than much of popular contemporary lyric poetry (Gioia, 2004, p. 13). Indeed, one can easily turn Augustan verse, say Alexander Pope's *Rape of the Lock*, complete with its heroic couplets, into a rap-like performance that sounds decidedly contemporary to student ears, even though it may appear visually inaccessible to students on the page. But performance poets rely on heavy doses of form, of music, to complete those auditory syntactic connections, and do not privilege the visual representation of the words on the page. Here semantic surprises underscored with an understandable rhythm create the joy inherent in not only the performance, but in the cleverness of the author's connections of rhyme, which are inchoate to the audience's life experience; they feel the meter and therefore it is well understood (Gioia, 2004).

Cowboy poetry, a genre that has thrived in the west, particularly in the rural, is a culturally native literary flora that appears dependent on ungulates, ballad rhythms, humor, and oral propagation. To take the metaphor one step further, the genre's genetic makeup may be so identifiable that poets without a particular social/work/geographic background would be naturally suspect, perceived as not genuine, and whose voice would be invalidated. Enthusiasm for cowboy ballads as a regional phenomenon comes with another caveat, especially for a teacher approaching the genre from outside the cowboy cultural milieu. Jim Blasingame (2007) writes that cowboy poetry "can not be separated from the culture it defines. Part of its value is in its power to define that culture and bind together the members who share an experience. It should not be taught as a novelty item" (p. 15). Here is an excerpt of a cowboy poem by Belt native Harold Anderson:

Deft Touch

Corral wall rail gapes wide away	A
Need not look far, on any day,	A
Something on a ranch needs repair.	B
Itchy neck on a tall bull,	C
Soughing winds that tug and pull,	C
Shoulder push from a prancy mare.	B
Could tie on a bale string noose,	A
But any nudge would drop it loose,	A
And split out the other end.	B
Larger spikes will firm it tight.	C
Ring shank grooves for a better bite.	C
Now's the time to make a mend . . .	B

In "Deft Touch," the line is primarily accentual meter, a meter that counts stress, not syllables. Even though the syllable counts are a fairly constant 7–8 per line, the poem's rhythm is dictated more by four strong stresses, or beats, on the majority of the lines. The rhyme scheme of AABCCB is an atypical ballad structure, and variations of ballad stanzas are often found in 'cowboy' poems (Gioia, 2004, p. 15).

The rhyme scheme of a typical ballad stanza is ABCB, where the second and fourth lines end with a strong end rhyme, as demonstrated in this stanza from "Ode to an Old Boot," also by Anderson:

There's a peculiar, perplexing quandary here.
It defies being understood.
How can anything look so terribly bad
and still feel so dog-gone good?

A traditional ballad stanza contains four lines of alternating tetrameter (four accentual beats) and trimeter (three beats). Usually the second and fourth line rhyme, but many variations are still considered ballads, and they may also contain these characteristics (Vendler, 1997, p. 74):

- A poem that tells a story.
- The story begins quickly, because the ballad is a condensed form of storytelling.
- The action in the stanzas are often more associative, rather than linear in narration; in other words, there is little connective language between them.
- They may contain a refrain.

Anderson's "Deft Touch" is a poem written for oral delivery, and the sophistication lies not just in its verse form, but in its use of jargon, idiomatic language, language that is, however, not didactic or pedantic. In short, the poem is immediately accessible due to its concrete, easily identifiable content (to the right audience), deprecating humor, and perhaps most important, as well as most formally characteristic, the poem's rhyme scheme. And one can imagine reading "Deft Touch" as a rap lyric just by replacing the content or social context; they are genetically similar in terms of rhythm and rhyme.

I'm beginning to suspect poetry better designed for performance is a key to popular public reading and has much to offer the students, and in Belt perhaps the ballad form of cowboy poetry would be most at home in the wider community. The problem is not with the form, nor with the more formal style, but with using the performance genre as a principal gateway into poetic exploration. My students approach poetry readings clearly from a performance rather than a generative point of view, and performances in class can quickly become parodic, where humor is found in the performance almost exclusively rather than as product of the text. Perhaps the reason is not the genre, but the cultural milieu, a lack of any deep connections with the text, oral or otherwise. In any case, performance as demonstrated by rap, slam, and cowboy poetry still seemed to me in the purview of shallow extrinsic motivation, and as a writer that privileges the internal, my instincts were still guiding me back to the intrinsic.

Writing for me is a visceral experience, much like that of an athlete (in training mostly), when the objectives, the text, at first seem out of reach, and then somehow, almost mysteriously, begin to align with one's expressive desires. In this way the music of a poem can reveal itself before the meaning reaches a satisfactory solution. This is why, I assume, a poem can resist completion for years, such as this example:

Hellgate Canyon Bridge

What approaches—leaves, dust along the banks
the span, cantilevered steeled-tense and braced
above stone-annealed river flanks.
Wood corked tight to suctioned sallow flows

of mist and oh so marvelous I turn to face
the rumbling windy river blow.
See the sunlight thread the girder's frames,
fall on fog and cloud and folding corvid wings,
unlike the quiet Corvus soaring southern spheres.

Canyon wind and river press and sift through the span—
a murmuring? Bridge bolt to buttress socked
in silt, but still a subtle motion through rail to hand—

a sense of slow time—glacial peaks froth
in chop like seas pressed to plain's sloping pier.

But is this thrumming caught with an iron net,
Or love, merging wind and river within a body's weir?

(Ross)

Compared to Anderson's "Deft Touch," a poem grounded in concrete imagery and purposeful action, "Hellgate," with its seemingly overly inflated language, ambiguous references, and not formal yet more obscure rhyme scheme, seems hopelessly out of place on 'main street' in Belt. And here the criticism lies squarely on the poem and not the street. Nevertheless, the reward of personally powerful language, even seemingly unfinished and ambiguous, can be manifestly physical, an emotive sense that underlies the intellectual; it is the satisfaction of creating language, expression that feels as much as it means, regardless of its aesthetic values (or lack thereof) to others or the intractability of its closure, or I would argue, even lack of a satisfactory understanding. So is there a 'most important' aspect when trying to teach writing and oral performance? In this example it is precisely the lack of closure that is important to the writer. The poem bumps up against the unknowable, clumsily perhaps, but a void that is formative because of what it lacks. This is where John Keats' famous aphorism of "negative capability," ". . . when a man is capable of being in uncertainties, mysteries, doubts, without any irritable reaching after fact and reason," becomes most important in my understanding of the poetic process (quoted in Adams, 1971, p. 494). And it is in and around these "uncertainties," "mysteries," and "doubts" where I will argue the most powerful intrinsic motivation for a writer often lurks; it is that moment of inspiration, that "AHA!" moment that is so critical for a writer's successful and pleasurable collaboration with one's internal muse.

In "Hellgate," and my explication thereof, I am demonstrating part of the divide that still separates my writing and analysis from the realm of the 'popular,' the accessible, the 'enjoyable,' poetry beyond a more academic setting. And the poem is not necessarily learned, perhaps just dense. I tend to burrow into the poetic project looking for hidden insights and connections, and then emerge, satisfied, and perhaps even somewhat smug with what minutia I have found. And the reader, regardless of experience, is still poking around on the surface seeking an entrance, an identifiable sound in the darkness. Enjoyable? Good luck! But the poet, critic, teacher in me says, "Wait a minute, it does rhyme, albeit rather oddly"; it does offer an oral direction. And the semantic, rhetorical fog, well, deal with it. The rhyme will still locate you within that ambiguity. But sitting in a fog is not the most enjoyable of experiences, not the best enticement, the best draw for an evening of poetry. So where does that leave us in terms of 'Belt it Out?' How and where do others willingly enter this poetic conversation?

Formalism is a style that is currently, as said before, generally out of fashion at the university level. 'New popular poets,' on the other hand, rely on heavy doses of form to complete those auditory, syntactic, and semantic connections. Here semantic surprises underscored with an understandable rhythm create the joy inherent in oral performance. So it's time to take another look at a viable and indigenous variety of poetry, that of the cowboy.

"He Cussed the Rain," another poem by Harold Anderson, demonstrates how rhyme functions in setting up anticipation and expectation in the listener, and then fulfills, satisfies that expectation. Using a sports analogy, imagine a basketball player practicing free throws where the first line of the rhyming couplet is the attempt, and the second, concluding rhyme is the ball going through the basket. Score! In this excerpt, three six-line stanzas containing three rhyming couplets each, most reinforced by end-stopped lines (commas or periods at the end of each line), provide a pleasurable experience for the listener and, I might add, the basketball shooter as well:

> . . . At dark Ron neared the canvas fly,
> Sparse barrier from the sluicing sky.
> Wet gloves, bogged boots and soggy hat,
> Soaked bone deep, a chilled water rat.
> Though drenched, he held a staunch abstain
> From comment on the sloshing rain.
>
> Then, Tall Tim bumped a canvas droop,
> Poured him a collar of iced sloop.
> The cow dog shook and sprayed his stew.
> He bent his head to sip his brew.
> The brim let go like a plugged drain,
> Filled his cup. Ron cussed, "Damn the rain."
>
> The crime produced an awesome hush
> As all had heard his rash outrush.
> The boss said, "Time you drew your pay.
> Stop by early, be on your way.
> When you first came I made it plain,
> That here you must not curse the rain . . .
>
> (p. 126)

Certainly in this poem (here heavily excerpted) Ron has reason to be annoyed with these seemingly innocuous aggravations, getting slopped with rainwater at every turn. And to be punished in such a severe manner for an offhand comment demonstrates that under this messy, quotidian, pastoral, cautionary tale are very formal relationships between cowboys, and more importantly, between cowboys and their working environment, an environment (in all its connotations) that is their unpredictable and serious host, the natural world itself. And again, I argue that it's the formal structure of the poem, the sympathetic rhythms of rhyme and meter that underscores these associations, parallels and reinforces these semantic relationships. Ron's hubris, his verbal mistake, doesn't interrupt the rhythm (and with 21 couplets, that's 21 'made' baskets in a row). For the listener (or basketball player), that's pleasurable indeed! But this is nothing new. Poets who appreciate formal structures have always understood the importance of music for meaning. So is there anything one can take away from this obvious analysis?

For poetry readings, for performance, regardless of genre, method, or style, perhaps a balance of 'music' and content is the best approach. In terms of music and rhythm, Jay Parini (2008) writes:

> The natural boundaries of verse preoccupy most poets, who gradually come to understand the useful and affirming limits of their art. Although most poetry written after the mid-twentieth century is 'verse free,' as anyone will know, I would argue that formless poetry does not really exist, as poets inevitably create patterns in language that replicate forms of experience.
>
> (p. xii)

That is a comforting notion, that all poetry, in a sense, is based on form, that the subtlest form, if true to experience, is never formless in its reception. So where in poetry is the pleasure located?

Robert Pinsky (1988), former poet laureate of the United States, a position that requires a political, promotional understanding of poetic discourse, writes, "If music's grace is the most basic aspect of a poem's appeal, and lively contextual sense is a poem's necessary social component, perhaps the most profound pleasure by which a poem engages our interest is by revealing to us the inward motion of another mind and soul" (p. 40). In this description, Pinsky offers a balance of music and content, where the internal lyrical sense is offered, released by the musical. Here, the "social component" is the western milieu of Montana landscape, economy, and quotidian art. And within this context, sharing a connection, a synapse between thought and word, derives pleasure. And as landscape engenders emotion, words communicate with the rhythms of the land. Perhaps then as these words make their way to the listener, it is incumbent on the writer to reprocess them with rhythm, the internal rhythms that were the precursors, the generators of the ideas themselves, musical representations of land and experience. But some poets, I suspect, may be too sensitive creating these internal rhythms, vibrations so weak and nuanced that their wavelengths don't reach the listener, unless that receiver is also hypersensitive to particular emotional/musical frequencies, or has the time and inclination to explicate them on the page.

Indeed, poetry can often sound aloof, exclusionary, as if some sort of intellectual token is needed to gain entry. In *Teaching Writing as Reflective Practice*, George Hillocks (1995) observes "many teachers of writing act as though writing is best done under some sort of compulsion, involving surrender to mysterious psychic powers" (p. 76). As an English teacher and poet, Hillocks' criticism is right on two counts. Art, creative composition, is often guided but not always explained by form, by prescription. So without the "mystery," would it cease to be art? His observation is also echoed by students who believe that good writers demonstrate innate abilities that cannot be learned, so why bother? This is a very debilitating perception in the classroom and tends to cut off any serious consideration students may have about their own writing, let alone sharing such perceived inadequacy with others in a public space. Demystification may be one mechanism of rhyme that I haven't sufficiently considered. Again, I can't seem to ignore or break free from the 'popular' poets.

How does one fit into a new community? This is an important question, perhaps even more important to a new teacher in the valley of a small, rural, Montana town, where that teacher ostensibly finds a niche, but is not sensitive to the underlying subtle, cultural differences that are magnified greatly in the lens of public performance. Cautions do abound. Michael Umphrey (2007), a teacher and director of the Montana Heritage Project, writes:

> If teachers believe that the place they have landed is so benighted that they are tempted to separate the kids from their local culture, I would suggest that instead they try to think of the entire community as the unit of educational change. Transforming a society tends to be more complex than we think it will be when we start out, and intellectuals don't, unfortunately, have a great track record at doing so directly—that is, by methods other than allowing the insights of scholarship to percolate through the culture.
>
> (p. 5)

Along with Umphrey's cautions about literary hubris, an academic pasteurization of indigenous social and literary culture, Keith Basso, writing from the perspective of an ethnologist studying Apache culture, makes pertinent observations on the 'outsider' that can be generalized to many localities. In "Wisdom Sits in Places," he writes:

> . . . the outsider must attempt to come to grips with the indigenous cultural forms with which the landscape is experienced, the shared symbolic vehicles that give shape to geographical experience and facilitate its communication— its re-creation and re-presentation—in interpersonal settings.
>
> (Basso, 1996, p. 56)

The language is academic, and deals directly with much wider cultural boundaries, but it is still relevant when considering a desire to help establish an accepted 'tradition' of any kind, especially one that apparently requires deep local affinities to be successful.

In the spirit of Basso's advice to "listen" to the community, I recall a conversation with a Belt resident when I first began discussing the idea of a public reading. She advised me to contact some local cowboy poets because they wrote "real poetry." Much of modern poetry "doesn't really say anything" I was told. Moreover, she regarded free verse as "feely" poetry, where emotions are not anchored to any concrete reality, and without end rhyme, lack an important marker of an identifiable poetic sensibility. It is instructive then that Harold Anderson's (2001) book of cowboy poetry, *A-Y Ranch Views 'N Verse*, begins with this introduction:

> The ranch is sliced into odd-shaped chunks by three paved highways, a rail-line and two creeks, Belt and Otter. Topography leans toward severe; sharp ridges, deep ravines, and steep slopes where thin soil barely hides underlying rock. Here and there, huge rocks protrude and dominate. Rim-rock streaks across steep faces above jumbled broken rock spills, homes for rock-chucks, pack rats, rattlers and bull snakes. Lovely scenery if you like naturally rough landscape, but pesky to move machines across and challenging for cattle to graze. Only a few acres along creek bottoms and sparse benches lie flat enough to till crops or cut hay. To some eyes it might look plumb ugly, but we love it.
>
> (p. iii)

Here, Anderson first grounds us in the geography. The prose is poetic, musical (especially lines 4–5), but with no overt references to the imaginative, the abstract. The descriptors are all concrete and physical, and the poetry, by inference, promises to rise off the land like dust, fog, sweat, and song. If Blasingame (2007) describes a genre inseparable from its culture, Anderson demonstrates again the synthesis, how quotidian human experience is inculcated in language by echoing off the land, a sound impossible to recreate without the imprint of a practicing rural livelihood. Perhaps 'invitation,' rather than 'promotion' is a better way of providing an element of local cultural authenticity, i.e., cowboy poetry, to the readings. Furthermore, cowboy is just one style of performance poetry, and homogeneity is not a quality one can use to describe a rural community like Belt. So what does one offer as a poetic model with local appeal so that it remains accessible to writers of all sensibilities? The answer may lie in combining the form of the cowboy poem, the traditional ballad stanza, with the interiority of the personal lyric, and as Basso would say, with "a sense of place."

In 1998 Mary Oliver wrote, "Poets no longer write ballads; they cannot since the world in which ballads were a rich, weird, and real part of everyday life no longer exists" (p. 52). Although she concedes that "literary ballads" are still written, I would argue that the folk ballad is far from dead. I use one of my own poems to help model a ballad form. "Picture of Sarah" is historically accurate, so it has familial importance. Here my great-great-grandmother Sarah McGuire's stern and distant countenance is part of her allure.

Picture of Sarah

    Eyes of chrysoberyl,
    kaolin skin cool as a cavern
    pictograph, her lips are pursed like
    caulked weathered planks.
    She is a vision from an Illinois **Altamira,**
    this arkosic tintype of
    Sarah Ann Chapman, Austin **McGuire.**

    Her father, a barrel
    maker, ripped staves from
    woodlots of virgin oak, pulled out
    stumps with chain and flare-eyed
    mules, piled them high into a gnarled **pyre,**
    the sparks dancing with
    Sarah Ann Chapman, Austin **McGuire.**

    Sarah married a young
    farmer. They built a clapboard

house, near a steeple-like
granite tor. But faith was no contract,
and he soon joined that wheezing winter **choir,**
leaving a hymnal for
Sarah Ann Chapman, Austin **McGuire.**

The year Sarah remarried, oil derricks
were jouncing thin steel proboscis
into the hills. And when he died,
she had enough. Drinking carbolic
acid, she made a request before she **expired:**
"bury me as I am," wrote
Sarah Ann Chapman, Austin **McGuire.**

In "Sarah," lines five and seven rhyme (see bold) in the refrain at the end of each stanza. Repetition provides, according to Samuel Taylor Coleridge, a "discharge of emotion that [can] not be exhausted in one saying" (quoted in Preminger, Warnke, and Hardison, 1974, p. 63). Refrains also build momentum, and in the final repetition, provide a release of that movement, adding closure. In "Sara," the refrain is a direct correlative of her life and experience. It's the building of a name, the building of history, of culture, of a past life in my present imagination. Orr (2002) writes that the story:

> ... of which personal memories are an excellent example, is one of imagina-
> tion's most basic ordering powers, a fundamental method of arranging the
> chaotic material of our experience into a form of meaning that emphasizes
> particular characters, specific details and actions—selected for their sym-
> bolic significance ... are crucial to our sense of self.
>
> (p. 19)

Sarah is resurrected from the dead, and her tragedy is understood within her name, imbued with the historical rhythm of the ballad. For students, the ballad can be the building of their own living histories, a history that celebrates their familial contribution to the wider culture. One assumption about the ballad's historicism is that "the work of an individual poet does not become a ballad until it is accepted by the folk and remodeled by the ballad conventions in the course of its tour in tradition" (Preminger et al., 1974, p. 63). As a literary definition, this sounds, well, academic, but perhaps we can make this working addition: In the ballad, the writer inhabits both the present and the past; she or he becomes both the receiver and the writer of tradition.

In reflecting on what might be learned from the characteristics of the previous examples, it is clear that these poems have varying degrees of auditory accessibility, characteristics that offer different levels of pleasure to a *listening* audience.

The inclusion of 'formal elements' (musical) appear to be a key to popularity, and that musicality, as provided by rhyme, meter, repetition, and narrative elements (preferably local), enhance the overall visceral (both semantic and musical) understanding and thus the pleasure these works provide in public recitation. In short, preparation and promotion for the readings should stress the musical, the rhythmic. Should these have been obvious points to anyone speculating on the success or failure of public performance? Perhaps, but they were not obvious to a university-trained writer and poet, one that privileges the personal over the social, the nuance in subject and form over the direct and overtly public.

If performance poetry's principal characteristic is a formal rhyme and meter, it represents a literary emphasis that has not been popular in recent years in university writing programs (Gioia, 2004, p. 11), including my experience as an MFA student at the University of Montana. Here one can sense the divide between the academic and the popular, and surely the academic model is one that I have principally employed in my classroom, perhaps to the detriment of generating interest outside the controlled learning environment of the classroom. Here, Umphrey's observations about literary hubris brings an awareness of not only the danger of an academic pasteurization of indigenous social and literary culture, but also the difficulty of a teacher, an outsider, trying to find entry into the local culture where the "insights of scholarship" can even find traction.

As an English teacher I often remind my students that poetry is meant to be heard, and yet as a writer, typically ensconced in the tight, solitary composition of the personal lyric, silent except for an imaginative orality, my emphasis had not been on hearing a poem. Furthermore, it's not enough for a writer and teacher to just intellectualize the egalitarian acceptance of local writing traditions; one must establish a personal aesthetic connection through poetic experience to be fully immersed in a community's poetic language. The object is to *experience* not just *explicate*. Perhaps the broader lesson is the necessity to explore not just the topography of local poetic/literary tradition from above, but kneel onto the cultural rhythms in the earth, the underlying structures that support the identity of writers in a community.

How does one fit into a rural community? This was the question that developed when trying to promote a public reading. While ostensibly creating a creative, academic niche, I was not sensitive to the subtle, underlying cultural preferences that are magnified greatly in the lens of public performance. I began to look at the tastes and sensibilities of my students and the Belt community at large. I found, with some hesitation I might add, a popular form of poetry, cowboy poetry, already embedded in the local literary geography. And the word 'geography' is important, for this is a genre that begins in the earth, the concrete (imagistically), and keeps a firm grasp on the physical, often the menial, the quotidian, a life that for many outsiders appears so Romantic.

In many ways the focus of this chapter has not been on a way to establish a poetic tradition, an authentic audience for student and community writers, but the evolution, the deconstruction of my bias as a writer, from poetry as primarily a vehicle of personal expression to that of a public discourse. Moreover, it is the musicality and local content of the poem that provides an oral connection to the audience, and thus the pleasure with the performance. The musical volume, as in meter and rhyme, it appears, must be raised to a higher level than I have been comfortable in the past. I have been resisting performance that is popular, such as performance, rap, cowboy poetry, poetry written to be understood viscerally, immediately, because it appeared to me to be shallow, simplistic, not tied to deeper meaning for the writer or the reader. And of course, overt simplicity does not mean a lack of sophistication.

Nevertheless, there is still abundant room for the quiet poems in public venues. Jonathan's poem "Of Patience" is particularly instructive. It is an example of a poem bridging the gap between poetry heavy on form containing end rhyme, and the subtly musical, with the use of anaphora, repetition, to set in motion the rhythmic dance with the audience. "Of Patience" also demonstrates that even with the personal lyric, the interiority of a writer's subject is often enhanced with the celebratory medium of music, and in a tenor that is as quiet or voluminous as a poem's agency demands. Robert Frost wrote that poetry is comprised of ideas revealed, as "when an emotion has found its thought and the thought has found words" (Frost and Untermeyer, 1963, p. 220), and by extension, those words then find voice in performance. The power "Of Patience" grows even stronger with that last auditory step.

Perhaps the word 'reader' is key to my misunderstanding of poetic, or any kind of *distinctively* oral, discourse. The difficulty to create interest in a public reading venue helped reveal my own limiting biases, and led to an adjustment of my understanding of what constitutes effective and meaningful poetic self-expression. And it is the redefinition of the slippery term 'literary' that encapsulates my adjustment from the university community, from the principally academic, to fully *hearing* the rural.

References

Adams, H. (1971). *Critical theory since Plato*. New York, NY: Harcourt Brace Jovanovich.

Anderson, H. (2001). *A-Y ranch views 'n verse*. Belt, MT: Harold and Meg Anderson.

Basso, K. H. (1996). Wisdom sits in places. In S. Feld & K. H. Basso (Eds.), *Senses of place* (1st ed.) (pp. 53–90). Santa Fe, NM: School of American Research Press.

Blasingame, J. (2007). *They rhymed with their boots on: Using cowboy poetry in the classroom.* Arizona English Teachers Association Convention.

Ellis, L., Gere, A. R., & Lamberton, L. J. (2003). Out loud: The common language of poetry. *English Journal*, 93(1), 44–49.

Frost, R., & Untermeyer, L. (1963). *The letters of Robert Frost to Louis Untermeyer* (1st ed.). New York, NY: Holt, Rinehart and Winston.

Gioia, D. (2004). *Disappearing ink: Poetry at the end of print culture*. Saint Paul, MN: Graywolf Press.

Hillocks, G. (1995). *Teaching writing as reflective practice*. New York, NY: Teachers College Press.

Oliver, M. (1998). *Rules for the dance: A handbook for writing and reading metrical verse.* Boston, MA: Houghton Mifflin.

Orr, G. (2002). *Poetry as survival.* Athens, GA: University of Georgia Press.

Parini, J. (2008). *Why poetry matters.* New Haven, CT: Yale University Press.

Pinsky, R. (1988). *Poetry and the world* (1st ed.). New York: Ecco Press.

Preminger, A., Warnke, F. J., & Hardison, O. B. (1974). *Princeton encyclopedia of poetry and poetics* (Enl. ed.). Princeton, NJ: Princeton University Press.

Reyes, G.T. (2006). Finding the poetic high: Building a spoken word poetry community and culture of creative, caring, and critical intellectuals. *Multicultural Education,* 14(2), 10–15.

Strever, I. A. (2006). "Who makes much of a miracle?" The evolution of a school's poetic culture. *English Journal,* 96(1), 66–69.

Umphrey, M.L. (2007). *The power of community-centered education: Teaching as a craft of place.* Lanham, MD: Rowman & Littlefield Education.

Van Wyhe, T.L.C. (2006). Remembering what is important: The power of poetry in my classroom. *English Journal,* 96(1), 15–16.

Vendler, H. (1997). *Poems, poets, poetry: An introduction and anthology.* Boston, MA: Bedford Books.

9

BRIDGING DIVIDES THROUGH PLACE-BASED RESEARCH, OR WHAT I DIDN'T KNOW ABOUT HUNTING IN THE NORTHERN ROCKIES

Hali Kirby-Ertel

GARDINER HIGH SCHOOL, GARDINER, MONTANA

The first writing assignment I gave to my tenth grade English students in Gardiner, Montana, was an argumentative essay on the topic of hunting. I began the day's lesson by handing out an article from *Time* magazine that was well balanced, but in general, opposed hunting. I would like to say I had no other motive than to use the article as a springboard for conversation and as a rhetorical model for writing their essays, but that simply is not true. A small part of me wanted to 'open the can' so to speak. But in the end, I opened the floodgates.

Initially, my attempts at prompting class discussion failed; the silence in the classroom was deafening. I tried again to stir my students by asking them to select portions of the text they found interesting or engaging, and share them with the class. This time, a firestorm of criticism exploded from the Gardiner students. Their criticisms ranged from the trouble with 'tree huggers' to the incompetence of the federal government. They attacked the media and the Park Service biologists, and, finally, they lashed out at me.

At the time, I didn't know Gardiner had been the mecca of elk hunting in Montana, and I didn't know every Gardiner kid in the class, both girls and boys, proudly filled their elk tag every year. I didn't know one's status could be based on the number and variety of wildlife one had hanging on her wall. I didn't know these things for a couple of reasons. First, I grew up on a farm in Iowa, during a time when you were more likely to be caught up in a tornado than see a deer in its natural habitat. My father hunted on occasion, and I remember him walking into our timber on frosty winter mornings, but the only things he bagged were peace and quiet. Second, and most importantly, I was so absorbed in my responsibility to teach English, that I didn't bother to consider the culture and values of the town I now called home or the students I had been charged to teach.

Looking back, my students' hunting heritage was obvious. I can recall being a little unnerved by the rifles resting in gun racks throughout the school parking lot and the laissez-faire attitude toward pocketknives attached to the kid's belt-loops. I was especially irked at the nine personal days granted to students for the purpose of hunting. Without realizing it, opening the can had put into question a way of life many of my students and their families valued. It put me in the position of outsider, a position that took years to leave behind.

My Context

Gardiner School has approximately 230 students K-12, and is situated along the north entrance to Yellowstone National Park. Gardiner is a class C school, a classification used by the state of Montana to group schools for athletic competitions. The state designates any high school with fewer than 119 students as a class C school. The school has a strong tradition in both academics and extracurricular activities. We have met our annual AYP (Annual Yearly Progress) goals each year and are the reigning state champs in volleyball and speech and drama. Through our successes in standardized testing and Advanced Placement scores, we have been designated by *USA Today* as the number one school in Montana two years running (US News and World Report, 2014).

Unlike many rural schools, we are well funded through federal monies designated for schools whose communities include federal land. Gardiner is surrounded by both a national forest and Yellowstone National Park (the Roosevelt Arch is visible from the front doors). It has been said that we live at the end of a 50-mile dead-end road, but that isn't quite true, at least not in the summer. Although remote, being 75 miles from the nearest shopping center, millions of people from all over the world find their way to Gardiner every year. My students, through jobs in restaurants and gift shops, as well as horseback riding and rafting guides, are exposed to a variety of regional and international cultures, so the sense of isolation isn't quite the same as in other rural communities in Montana. Much of our success can be attributed to our ability to retain teachers and provide a variety of courses to meet the diverse needs of our students, none of which would be possible without the additional federal dollars we receive each year.

Our school history is rich and complicated, like most schools that have evolved through consolidation. At the turn of the twentieth century, six country schools dotted the southern portion of Park County, Montana. Gradually, as travel from the outlying communities to Gardiner became more convenient, these one-room schoolhouses began to close, making way for the Gardiner School District. Consolidation was necessary and therefore accepted, but the K-6 Mammoth School (erected in 1962) remained open through the 2007–08 school year.

Mammoth Hot Springs, the headquarters for Yellowstone National Park, is comprised of upper-division employees of the National Park Service and Xanterra Parks and Resorts (a private company contracting the hospitality services in

Yellowstone and other national parks). Nearly all of these families are transplants from around the country. Because of this, their sense of place and what this place means to them can be quite different. For transplants, Gardiner is a temporary space. It is not where they are from, it is where they live. While they certainly value the beauty and history of the Park, they aren't necessarily interested in fostering local values. They bring with them their own values, which is wonderful in that it brings diversity to our community, but it also brings friction. In contrast, the locals are as rooted to the place as the sage that dot the landscape; Gardiner is not a stepping stone for them, it's a place to grow. With this rootedness comes a natural resistance to change, especially from outside influences. This tension between the old and the new—the locals and the transplants—keeps the wheels turning in the greater Gardiner community.

The rift between residents of the Park and Gardiner began before 1872, when Yellowstone became a park, but it really heated up early in the twentieth century, when Mammoth residents sought federal funding for a new school. Mammoth residents are not Montana citizens; they are residents of Wyoming. As such, they have no legal right to vote in Gardiner school board elections, and the nearest Wyoming district is more than a three-hour drive from Mammoth. Though the federal government is required to provide Park Service employees across the country with adequate schooling for their children, most national park employees send their students to schools in bordering communities.

According to Park documents, in the late 1930s, "Mammoth residents expressed concerns that they were unable to have input in the ways in which their children were educated, unable to elect their own representatives to a local school board, and were ill served in a discrepancy of educational expectations between the people of Gardiner and the people of Mammoth" (Whittlesey, 2008, p. 8). The Park parents' resistance to schooling their children in Gardiner led Park officials to push the federal government for monies to erect a school in Mammoth (p. 4). Park officials explained that, "while there was both a grade school and a high school at Gardiner, it was very crowded and quite primitive" (p. 5). Five miles separate Mammoth and Gardiner, a distance, in the opinions of many Gardiner residents, unsubstantial enough to warrant a separate school. The construction of a new school in Mammoth built an even bigger wall between the two communities.

When I began teaching in Gardiner back in 1999, my students would refer to one another as either Gardiner students or Mammoth students, even though all of them attended Gardiner School. It was the equivalent of the Jets and Sharks in a small Montana town. Bridging this gap became one of my primary goals. How can I help transplant students appreciate their new home and facilitate acceptance from the local students? How do I help the local students share with transplanted students their values in a way that is productive and nonthreatening? How do I facilitate community in an English class? Unfortunately, the school debate was but only one rift between the Gardiner and Park residents. The longer I taught in Gardiner, the more I understood the complex relationship between these two communities.

More of the Story

When I developed my argument unit on hunting, I had no idea of the war that waged between the Gardiner and Mammoth communities since the initiation of the 1995 wolf relocation project. I had not been witness to the community meetings where Gardiner residents showed up in mass shouting to the winds, "The only good wolf is a dead wolf!" I didn't witness the Park superintendent and biologists explaining the science behind their decision or the overwhelming public support across the nation. The people had spoken. But the people closest to the issue; the people who prized local control above all else; the people whose livelihood and heritage were at stake, would be outvoted. I did not read the letters to the editor where Gardiner residents defended the heritage of hunting and the economic impact the reintroduction project would have on their families. The article from *Time* magazine that I selected to initiate class discussion talked about hunting safety and the ethics of big game hunting around the globe. It cited examples of inexperienced hunters mistaking women wearing white gloves for white-tailed deer, it mentioned the importance of culling herds of deer to keep them out of suburban communities, and it questioned the existence of trophy hunting and its role in perpetuating the poaching of animals for their antlers and tusks. While hunting safety and wildlife management are two universal issues all hunters value, they were not the key issues within *my* community.

Early that fall, before I assigned the essay and as elk hunting season approached, my students asked me if I hunted. Of course, my answer had been no and probably included something about my aversion to killing animals. In response, they challenged me to defend my stance, and I didn't like it. As I shared my reasons, they dismissed them as quickly as they left my mouth. I felt bullied, and I knew there were students in the room who felt very similar to me. So, when I developed this unit, I had hoped to challenge my students to think critically about hunting, to really question something that seemed to them to be unquestionable. Unfortunately my unit became as one-sided as my kids' attitude toward hunting. It appeared to my Gardiner students that I was forcing an anti-hunting agenda on them, and it appeared to my Mammoth students that I viewed their values as superior. I had kids fighting and parents calling, and a divide between the Gardiner and Mammoth students, which I was completely unaware of, took on Grand Canyon-like proportions.

My naïveté, I'm sure, seems questionable. I had lived in Montana for over two years when I assigned this essay, but I had been living within the boundaries of Yellowstone National Park, surrounded by a coterie of naturalists and biologists whose focus was on wildlife conservation and sustainability through a natural relationship between predators and their prey, rather than through human culling. Their values became my values. Like me, they were not from Montana and hunting had never been part of their culture. I didn't value the skill and artistry required to ethically hunt large game, because I saw nothing ethical about a game of chase between a gun wielding hunter and his unarmed prey. Hunting appeared barbaric and unnecessary. I let my personal beliefs distract me from the real purpose of teaching, which is to give students the means and the time to fully investigate issues important to them, empowering them to draw their own conclusions.

After my hunting essay debacle, I chose safer topics for student research, topics that rarely caused a ripple in the Gardiner community: the death penalty, the lottery, video games, the drinking age, etc. My students dutifully went through the motions of writing these essays, and I dutifully read them. Together we walked this comfortable path, and we missed out on opportunities to think about and reason through issues that matter most to us.

My History

In the fall of 1999, I began teaching English at Gardiner School in Gardiner, Montana. I was not a first-year teacher, since I had spent two prior years teaching high school English on the Northern Cheyenne Indian Reservation in Lame Deer, Montana, where chronic poverty and a significant lack of resources made teaching difficult. Lame Deer was rural and remote, just like Gardiner, but the experience I gained on the reservation didn't transfer to this white, middle-class school. So though I had two years teaching under my belt, like most first-year teachers, I felt overwhelmed. I was instantly buried in what seemed like an insurmountable pile of work. I taught English 8, 9, 10, JH and HS Speech and Drama, Yearbook, and Creative Writing. Preparing lessons and assessing students in seven different classes, while at the same time coaching varsity volleyball, left me little time to take in my surroundings. I worked. I worked hard and long, but no matter how hard I worked I never felt good about my teaching.

Unlike some rural schoolteachers, I did have a colleague. Mrs. Olig taught seventh, eleventh, and twelfth grade English in my school; she also taught Spanish I and II and worked as the high school's guidance counselor. But there was little to no time to collaborate. Our prep periods were at different times, and our school had not built in any professional development days for collaboration.

The accountability to my students and to the Gardiner community weighed heavily on me as an early career teacher. I felt a lot of pressure to live up to the high standards the Gardiner community expected of its school. I was replacing an English teacher who had failed at maintaining those high standards, and since there weren't state standards at that time, and I never found a written curriculum in my classroom, I really didn't know what constituted high standards.

As I tried to find my way, I let my own stereotypes of rural education play into how and what I taught my students. As a graduate of a rural school where writing instruction was nonexistent, I assumed the weaknesses in instruction I experienced as a student were likely the weaknesses of all rural schools. So, I asked my students to write. Well actually, during those early years, I *told* them to write. Writing was like a bitter pill I made my students swallow every day, under the 'Trust me, I know what's best for you' banner. I remember saying things like, "When you leave here and you join the real world, you will realize the importance of strong writing skills."

In those early years teaching in Gardiner, I dedicated myself to preparing my best and brightest students for a real world in large cities, where important people go to do important things. It did not occur to me that my good intentions only diminished the value of my students' community. My campaign instilled in them that successful people don't live in places like Gardiner; successful people go else-where. And even though I knew of very few unemployed parents, and my husband and I both have careers we love, I continued to push my agenda.

Unfortunately, encouraging students in rural schools to believe that returning to their rural roots is a sign of failure is a common practice of educators in America. Stereotypes about being behind the times, or outright backward, are forced upon people in rural communities by outsiders who believe they know best. I'm not sure if my air of superiority was an attempt at masking my lack of confidence as a young teacher or if I truly believed I was better than the people of Gardiner. Either way, my arrogance, whether actual or only perceived, made adapting to my new community even harder.

The most important thing I have learned is that my best teaching has come from my greatest failures. I have failed a lot over the course of 14 years, but I don't sweat the failures anymore, because with each failure I become better. After licking my wounds and taking part in a substantial amount of self-reflection, I realized my hunting experiment had a lot of potential. No other assignment I gave that year prompted such an electric response from those tenth graders. I had something with the topic of hunting, but I needed help navigating this volatile issue with a little more sophistication.

Professional Development

For me, life as a rural teacher is isolated, not only geographically but professionally, too. My experience with high quality professional development has been hit or miss. Early in my career, I was overwhelmed with the responsibility to develop curricula for each of my seven classes. Literature textbooks and a smattering of novels were waiting for me in my classroom closets, but how, when, and to whom I should teach these texts? Surely, guidance would come from the district administration or the other English teacher.

My first professional development experience in Gardiner took place two days before students arrived for the school year. Those two days consisted of trainings for CPR and First Aid, blood-borne pathogens, and FERPA (Family Educational Rights and Privacy Act); a meeting with the athletic director to discuss my coaching duties; and an all-staff welcome back, 'Have a Good Year' sendoff from my superintendent. Strangely enough, after all these years of teaching in Gardiner, the two PIR days before school are exactly the same every year.

Though my school's in-service program was lackluster, I had high hopes for outside professional development specific to the task of teaching Language Arts. Each year in mid-October, the state holds a two-day conference where teachers and other education professionals present workshops in all disciplines. My first year, the conference was held in Billings, Montana, 170 miles from Gardiner. Each session is generally 50–100 minutes long, and though teachers from across the state are encouraged to submit proposals, it has been my experience that most teacher-presenters are from the urban clusters located around the conference site.

These were some of the best teachers in the state, but their teaching contexts were different from mine: Billings, the biggest city in Montana, is like a metropolis compared to Gardiner. These teachers taught ninth grade English all day, or they specialized in creative writing. Their classes were large and formed in some way through tracking. I was teaching *Julius Caesar* to everybody, while they only taught it to honor students. Many of their classes were just one semester long and they rarely taught the same student twice. I taught the same students all year for three years in a row. It only makes sense their demonstration lessons were designed around their context, but when I packed up their lessons and brought them back to my students in Gardiner, they never quite jived without a lot of adaptation.

The state teaching conference had fulfilled my 'Hows' (How do I teach persuasive speaking? How do I conduct literature circles?), and I walked away with a backpack loaded with lessons for speech and drama, poetry, literature, grammar, and creative writing, but all those sessions failed to show me why? Why am I teaching these concepts in this particular way? Why is this information important for *my* students? It felt good to have some ammunition as I returned to my classroom, and I quickly implemented all I had learned, but my lessons lacked cohesion and a long-term vision.

For my first five years of teaching, professional development offerings looked very much the same: housekeeping procedures, meetings, and public health trainings were offered through the school. And each October, I made the trek to the state conference to restock my arsenal of creative, yet completely unrelated, lessons. The lack of direction for teaching English to *everyone* began taking its toll. Hard work wasn't enough; I needed some legitimate guidance if I hoped to continue teaching.

It was in that fifth year, which was in fact the very year I considered abandoning the teaching profession, that my principal sent me an e-mail seeking applications for a grant conducting oral history projects. It was through the Montana Heritage Project, a place-based research and writing initiative developed by the Montana Historical Society and sponsored by the Liz Claiborne and Art Ortenberg Foundation. It was a $2,000 opportunity to fund local, student-led research, but more importantly it was my opportunity to work with and learn from some of the top teachers from rural communities around the state. I was awarded a grant in the spring and was invited to attend the annual

Heritage Festival, where students from every Heritage Project site presented their research to an audience made up of their peers and other teachers and volunteers with the project.

During the summer, I attended a fully funded, week-long workshop on the theory behind place-based learning and the nuts and bolts for conducting oral histories. Heritage Project teachers and members of the Montana Historical Society conducted the workshops. I was given the tools and inspiration to begin Gardiner's first oral history project, but just as important, I now had a group of mentors ready to answer my questions.

My first oral history project was born from the results of that first argumentative essay. Six years later, after attending the Heritage Project's summer institute, I asked my students to learn before they argued. The overarching theme to our research became the history of hunting in the greater Gardiner area. After spending 30 minutes at home researching our topic, it soon became apparent to my students that Google wasn't going to be much help when researching local history. I knew the Internet wouldn't be helpful, but I wanted my students to take their typical path to research, so we could discuss other ways to collect information. We discussed the value of learning from our families, friends, and community. By the end of the class period, we had made a list of possible interview subjects, ranging from hunters, hunting guides, business owners, biologists, environmentalists, and historians. I wanted to be sure we considered as many angles on the topic as possible. I wanted my students to not only hear things they agreed with, but also to hear things that challenged their beliefs.

Throughout the years, students from Gardiner found themselves interviewing adults from the Park on contentious topics such as the Park Service's "Let it Burn" policy and the 1995 wolf reintroduction. In addition, Mammoth students found themselves interviewing hunting guides and ranchers on the very same issues. Students were forced to look at issues from all perspectives, and many of them found life isn't as black and white as it once appeared. As a result, my students were more open-minded on a lot of topics; I only had to remind them of their experiences with the oral history project.

Additionally, interviewing Gardiner and Mammoth residents brought our community closer. Adults, mostly the elderly, who had not previously been in the school or hadn't visited in a long time, found the energy from the school and its students agreed with them. They became our biggest advocates in times when community support for the school was lacking. We have preserved their interviews and transcriptions in the school library, community library, the National Park Service's Heritage Center, and the National Archives; developed community presentations honoring their contributions; but more importantly, we have told their stories. All involved have created a historical record of a time and place that will no longer be forgotten. Since I began conducting oral histories, we have lost five of our previous contributors, and I am thankful we took the time to learn from them, to catalogue their perspective on Gardiner's past, present, and future, not only for my students but for the contributors' families and future generations.

Inserting oral histories into my curriculum was as much for me as it was for my students. Developing localized research projects and interviewing locals on issues close to them put me in position to join the community. I was no longer viewed as an outsider, and even though I didn't always see eye to eye with them on every issue, I felt accepted. I think locals and transplants alike were pleased that the children of Gardiner were not only learning about controversial topics around the globe but also about the ones in their own backyard.

Healthy communities are developed when the people living in them are invested in identifying problems and seeking solutions through community-wide dialogue. These authentic research and writing experiences have become essential in turning my student inquiry projects into work worth doing. The interview is only one component of an oral history project. Students use other primary and secondary resources to augment the transcriptions and to develop a comprehensive understanding of the overall topic. For the most part, the Internet is insufficient in providing them with the information they seek. Instead, students' paths to knowing take them to local and college libraries, museums, local landmarks, and to people's homes, all to search for books, old newspapers, journals, and artifacts. Knowledge is tangible and it is valued.

The Heritage Project was my first taste of teacher collaboration, and my first professional development piece to last longer than three hours. It was not the fly-by professional development I had experienced at the state conference. Rather than incorporating a smattering of isolated lessons throughout the school year, I could build my curriculum using the principles of place-based education. I met with the Heritage Project teachers three more times over the course of the following school year. All workshops were two days and held in Helena, Montana, a three-hour drive from Gardiner, so I missed about nine days of school that year to attend those workshops. After attending a summer institute held by the Montana Heritage Project, I began to conduct oral history projects within my English 9 and 10 classes. Over the years we have completed several projects, ranging from our school's history to economic and environmental effects from the 1988 Yellowstone fires.

Unfortunately, following my first year with the Project, the financial supporters pulled the funding on the decade-old project. Without the funds to pay for travel and substitutes, schools could not afford to support the professional development aspect of the Heritage Project. Teachers continue to conduct and submit oral history projects to the Montana Historical Society, and some teachers keep in touch through a listserv, but the Heritage Project as a whole is not sustainable without financial backing. Teachers farthest from Helena find it too challenging to maintain a connection with the project. Though my time with the Project was cut short, I came to understand the value of collegiality, of self-directed research, and the promise of time and a little bit of money to turn theory into practice.

Conclusion

As a first-year teacher in a rural school, it would have been nice to receive a handbook from the administration including the family trees of the long-standing families in Gardiner, the values that separate and divide the community, or even the best place to get a burger. But they didn't, and I'm not sure I would have listened anyway. It's like in *To Kill a Mockingbird*, when Miss Caroline, Scout's first grade teacher unknowingly shames Walter Cunningham Jr., by trying to give him a nickel for lunch. Of course, if she had only listened to Scout, she would have gracefully navigated through the complicated social norms of Maycomb, AL. The lesson in *To Kill a Mockingbird* for all teachers, but most importantly for teachers in rural areas, is to try to learn before you teach. Miss Caroline, in her peppermint-striped dress, saw it as her duty to civilize those children. She did not recognize the possibility that they could teach her something. I made the same mistake.

Today, I am in my fourteenth year of teaching at Gardiner Schools, and though I still feel accountable to my students and my community, that weight no longer seems as daunting. In order to be successful, I had to become more than a school employee; I had to become a member of the community. My teaching needed to reflect the cultural values of the community and provide my students with the knowledge and skills necessary to live in a global society. These 14 years have been challenging, but through shifting my pedagogy and incorporating place-based education into my curriculum, I have found peace with my teaching and a home in the Gardiner community.

References

US News and World Report. (2014). Best high schools: Special report on education. Retrieved June 5, 2014, from www.usnews.com/education/.

Whittlesey, L. H. (2008). *A brief history of the school at mammoth hot springs, Yellowstone National Park, Wyoming*. National Park Service.

10

WHOSE KIDS ARE THEY, ANYWAY? BALANCING PERSONAL AND PROFESSIONAL IDENTITIES IN A RURAL SCHOOL

Kari Patterson

FAIRFIELD HIGH SCHOOL, FAIRFIELD, MONTANA

I was convinced from an early age that I had been switched at birth; I had no doubt I was supposed to have been raised on a ranch. I was horse crazy from the time, as a three-year-old, I rode a Shetland pony at a circus. Unlike most girls who eventually transfer this obsession to boys, I never outgrew it. I begged for a horse and took it as a "yes" whenever my father said "we'll see." Finally a friend told me that I always said I was getting a horse but never actually got one. I didn't ask my dad again. Instead, I looked to my next option. When I grew up, I would tell my Uncle Olaf, I was going to marry a rancher and live in the foothills of the Bridger Mountains, twenty miles from his home in Belgrade, Montana. Toward that end, I set my sights on going to college at Montana State University, which was even closer to those mountains.

As love would have it, however, I married a longtime friend who was studying to be an engineer. I was overjoyed when we received a horse as a wedding present, but it didn't look like I was going to get my ranch. After we graduated from college, my husband wanted to move back to our hometown of Great Falls so he could work with his father. I had never really cared for Great Falls, probably just because it was too familiar, and was not looking forward to the prospect of going back. I consented, however, with the contingency that we would not have to *really* live in Great Falls.

To hedge my bets, I started applying for teaching jobs within a reasonable driving distance of Great Falls. I applied to one school where the principal admitted that, though my transcripts looked good, my lack of basketball experience was a major drawback. (They ended up hiring a woman who had been an English major with me, had gotten lukewarm grades, but had played college ball.) Then I applied for an English teacher/wrestling coach position. I wrote in my cover letter that, "though I have no wrestling experience, I am willing to learn." Not surprisingly, I wasn't called for an interview. I'm red in the face now just thinking about it.

Then a position opened up in Augusta, a dusty town of fewer than 300 people on the east slopes of the Rockies that is home to what is arguably the wildest rodeo in the state. Since the enrollment was so small, the opening was for a teacher who would cover English in grades 7–12. Six preps per day would be a big load, I knew, but I didn't care. I wanted to live in Augusta, the Gateway to the Bob Marshall Wilderness Area.

I came to the interview ready to impress in a pastel-striped blouse, pink culottes (think 1980s), and stiletto heels. The school board members, on the other hand, came straight to the interview from setting dams in their fields and were wearing irrigation boots and flannel shirts. I rattled off my qualifications and expounded my philosophies and didn't get the job.

I was despondent. I wanted that job so badly and felt sure that I had nailed the interview. I couldn't get over the rejection, so, in a move very uncharacteristic of me, I called the chairwoman to find out why I hadn't been selected. In a motherly voice she told me that I had made it to the top two. In making their final determination, however, she said that they had felt I wouldn't be happy with rural life and, therefore, had chosen the other finalist, a man from a small town in eastern Montana.

The school year was fast approaching, and I had pretty much decided that my chances of securing a position for fall were nonexistent. I figured I would sign up to substitute teach in Great Falls and bide my time until spring. But then a job came looking for me. I had virtually forgotten that I had sent query letters to all the rural schools surrounding Great Falls when my husband first told me that he wanted to move home. Most of the schools I wrote to had not been advertising openings, but I thought it couldn't hurt to get my name out there. As it turned out, a junior high teacher in Fort Shaw had been offered a position in Great Falls one week before school started, and administration was left shorthanded in the last minute. With no time to recruit candidates, they looked through the applications they had on file, including my unsolicited transcripts, and asked if I could come to the school the next day. This time, I wore a more conservative outfit to the interview, settled into my down-home Montana drawl, and got the job.

Fort Shaw is not the image of the West that Augusta is. Not now, anyway. It had been a military outpost in the 1880s. It was then converted to an Indian boarding school, which earned the impressive distinction of having the world champion girls' basketball team in 1904. Now, however, it is not much more than a small clutch of homes and the school. My students' parents generally commuted to Great Falls for work or were farmers and ranchers. Travelers on the highway that cuts through town have no reason to stop in Fort Shaw, but I was glad to have it as my destination.

Once the excitement of securing a job passed, however, it was replaced with panic about actually teaching. I remember driving to school that first day, envying the cows in the field that had nothing to do but eat and sleep their lives away. I remember being sick to my stomach as I waited for the bell to ring. What was I going to do after I introduced myself and the students sat silently staring at me, waiting for me to line out the day, to know all the answers? Before I could faint, however, the seventh graders tumbled in, loaded with questions and pouring out information about themselves. I remember the great relief I felt that morning when it hit me that these weren't the theoretical *students* I had been studying in college. They were just a bunch of kids; I could just be myself. Everything was going to be all right.

Though I am only certified to teach English and reading, I was assigned English, reading, science, art, home economics, physical education, health, and, worst of all, cheerleading. Being required to teach several subjects is not uncommon in a rural school, but this was quite a stretch. Suddenly, the six English preps at Augusta weren't sounding too bad. With so many classes to manage, I took comfort in telling myself that junior high is about teaching children more than it is about teaching subjects. I do believe that is true, but only if it is seen as a reason to nurture the child and not as an excuse for teaching poorly. I used it for both.

Admittedly, I put most of my energy into reading and writing that first year, but I did a decent job with the other subjects, too, with the exception of science. My qualifications there did not go beyond high school biology, and what I remembered from it did not last more than a few weeks. After that, I would go home at night and ask my husband to explain, say, electricity to me. The next day, I would give a lecture in a confident tone and then hurry on to the next subject before the smart kids could have a chance to formulate questions. It was stressful for me and a disservice to my students. Thankfully, I swapped science for sixth grade English the next year, so damages were limited.

I also found myself overwhelmed with papers to correct. I was so afraid of having an unfilled moment of class time that I made sure to have assignments backed up end to end. Commendable as that may seem, it was an impossible thing to perpetuate for long. After school, I would first prepare another full load of work for the next day. By the time I had that done, it would be dark, so I would pack up the papers that needed correcting and drive the 30 miles home. After fixing dinner, I would intend to tackle the papers but simply could not make myself. I felt that, once I sat down, I had to finish the entire stack. This thought absolutely drained me of energy, and I would correct none of them. The mountain grew and grew, and I became depressed. I honestly developed a sort of tunnel vision so I could not see that paper beast sitting on the table. Exhausted by the weight of unfinished work, I started going to bed earlier and earlier every night.

Finally, I realized I had to do the unthinkable and ask for help. I took the pile down to the principal's office after school one day and revealed my shame and despair. He smiled sympathetically at my plight and said, "Go through the pile. Decide what the students really need to get back. Throw the rest away. From now on, don't give a writing assignment until you get the last one corrected. Never let this happen again." I gratefully took his advice. The kids never asked about any of the busywork I threw away.

Another challenge that year was that my eighth graders did not particularly care for me. They had loved the teacher I replaced, and they took it out on me when she 'abandoned' them to move on to a class AA school. I was nothing more than an evil stepmother, and they were going to be sure I knew I was no substitute for their *real* teacher. The girls—make that six of the *cheerleaders*—were especially hard on me right from the start. Seven girls wanted to be on the squad and I had seven outfits, so I said they could all be cheerleaders. Six of them did not want the seventh on the team, so they demanded that I hold tryouts and that someone be cut. When I told them that was not going to happen, they recruited every girl in the junior high to say that, since auditions were not required, they all wanted to be cheerleaders. Not wanting to miss a teachable moment, I explained to them that they were demonstrating what *catty females* are. But, I'm proud to say, we had seven cheerleaders that season. Years later, one of these girls told me about how they had all gotten together at recess to come up with a way to make me cry. I told her that I remembered crying once. "No," she said, "you don't understand. *Every day* we would try to make you cry." Gosh. And they looked so sweet in those uniforms.

But my seventh graders, oh, my seventh graders, they were another story. They had not had my predecessor, so I was not the embodiment of rejection for them. Instead, we got along like a family. We told endless stories about our lives. We read *Treasure Island* and *Huckleberry Finn*. We bound books and filled them with their writings. We had a contest to see who could come up with the best breakfast drink. We buried a time capsule. We snapped our fingers in appreciation of each other's beatnik poetry. We had fierce battles of dodge ball. We played follow-the-leader, jumping from boulder to boulder and scurrying across fallen logs along a creek. I set a brilliant girl free through independent studies. I gave a troublemaker a new start by ignoring the reputation that preceded him. I found the pranksters hilarious and the wallflowers adorable. It was love all around.

When they graduated after our two years together, I was hugely pregnant with my first child and distraught that my little darlings were marching out of junior high. They were glad to be moving on to high school, so they were all smiles as they greeted family and friends in the receiving line—until I came along. I started crying before I reached the first kid and didn't stop until I got home. And it wasn't a dainty little sniffle. This was a belly-jiggling, chin-warbling, snot-running wail. While I buried my face into the shoulder of one student, the next would be bracing himself, thinking, "Shoot, man, she's coming for me next!"

I blamed it on a hormonal imbalance caused by the pregnancy. But I remember very well the real reason I had cried. I had let myself become too attached to those kids. I had harbored their secrets, shielded their bruises, eased their awkwardness. I had needed them to need me, to validate me as a teacher, and they had. But, like an inexperienced foster mother, I had foolishly forgotten that they weren't mine to keep. I remember being jealous of their parents who were not losing their children but were moving on with them to the next stage in life. They looked so smug as they laid claim to their sons and daughters at the end of the evening and left me behind with an empty classroom. I knew I couldn't go through that year after year.

As it turned out, I didn't have to. My daughter was born in the fall, and we moved, in fulfillment of my dream, to a beautiful old homestead outside the town of Fairfield. I was more than happy to focus my attention on my daughter and my home, so I quit my job. When Hannah was a year old, however, my principal asked me to come back. Fort Shaw had consolidated with the neighboring town of Sun River, so I would only have to teach English. I took the job and things were going well.

My son Chas was born the following summer, and when school began again in the fall, I soon found that I was trying to do too much. I would stumble out of bed at 4:30, get myself ready, get Hannah and Chas up at 6:00, get them ready, drive 30 miles to Sun River, take the kids to the babysitter, go to work, pick up the kids, drive back home, cook dinner, do some housework, correct papers, spend 'quality' time with my children, say a few passing words to my husband, fall into bed, and start again a few hours later.

I couldn't keep doing it. I remember praying for help, for more time with my children. My prayer was answered, unfortunately, when five-month-old Chas was diagnosed with leukemia. I guess I should have been more specific about my plea for time. I quit my job immediately and spent the next four years keeping him alive. School was far from my mind as I put all my energy into his survival, and, hallelujah, he made it. Needless to say, my priorities were changed. We had another son, and my husband and I decided that I should stay home with our kids until the youngest was in kindergarten. I stretched that out a bit and didn't return to the classroom full-time for 12 years. I've never regretted it.

I teach high school in Fairfield now, and my relationship with my students is different than it was with that first class of seventh graders. Every spring I watch my seniors graduate, and I rarely cry when they swing their tassels to the right sides of their caps. I don't like to think that it's because I've become hardened, but I do know that I see things differently at 55 than I did at 26. For one thing, I have become more of a stoic in my acceptance of change. Kids grow up and move on. That's life. Plus, I remember being their age. As I recall, the stage of life they are entering is much easier than the one they are leaving behind, so I am honestly happy for them when they move on. For another thing, I have three kids of my own now. That's plenty.

What I remember now that I hadn't understood with that first class is that the students are not my children; they belong to their parents. And, rather than resenting their claim to them, I defer to it. Now I just want to be their teacher. I consider it my job to make the high school years a guided tour toward independence. I help the students see that, to learn, they have to ask questions; that mistakes are necessary for gaining wisdom; that research leads to informed decision making;

that effort and planning result in quality work; that with freedom comes responsibility; and that they need to clean up after themselves when they make messes. Oh, and, of course, I teach them to read and write. These are the skills I have been entrusted with, and they are enough. In the end, I want them to be able to continue their educations for the rest of their lives without me. With that in mind, I keep my objectives broad. I consider it my responsibility to provide a framework for their learning. I do not believe it is my job to be their interior decorator; that job belongs to parents.

Eleven years ago, when I applied for the job I currently hold, the superintendent asked me what I wanted my students to think of me. It was a pretty standard question that I had replied to with a generic, idealistic answer many times before. This time, though, I hesitated, mouth literally agape, and could not bring myself to proclaim that I wanted to be their role model. My word, who wants that responsibility? I felt like Charles Barkley, who once said, "I am not a role model. . . . Parents should be role models. Just because I dunk a basketball doesn't mean I should raise your kids" (Barkley, 1993). Who, more than a parent, should be the reason kids love what they love, hate what they hate, believe what they believe? After too long a pause, I finally told him I didn't know what I wanted them to think of me: that I could teach reading and writing, I guess. He shrugged that that was fair enough.

Though I stumbled upon that answer at the time, I embrace it now. I feel that a teacher's job is to give students the tools they need to expand their minds, not personal ideologies that narrow them. Benjamin Bloom's (1956) hierarchy for teaching lends itself to this same philosophy. The base of his pyramid is knowledge, and it is important to notice that that base is broad. It should be as broad as reading with comprehension and writing with clarity. We want students to comprehend, apply, analyze, synthesize, and evaluate information. We have to remember to keep our focus on *how* to question more than on *what* to question. I don't mean to sound sinister. Teachers aren't generally scheming to take over the world. But we do wield an awful lot of power from the podium. And it doesn't have to be blatant indoctrination. In fact, it is with subtlety, with the casual comment, that we are generally the most convincing. I know I have heard students repeat verbatim, with the conviction of lifelong beliefs, what I have said in class that morning.

Several years ago, I was made painfully aware of the impact of my opinions. A friend had bought an appaloosa from a former student of mine I'll call Ann. My friend didn't have a horse trailer to haul it in, so I volunteered to go with her to pick up the mare. I was impressed by the horse's calm disposition and sound confirmation, especially since I knew Ann was selling her for little or nothing. I asked her why she was letting her go, and she said she had never really liked the horse. I asked her why, and she said it was because of me. *Me?* What had I done? The day in middle school when she got the horse, she said, she had been ecstatic. Knowing that I loved horses, she had come straight to my room to tell me the big news. After sharing in her excitement, I apparently added that I had never cared much for appaloosas, with their skimpy tails and albino eyes. That's all it took. I don't even remember saying it—although it's true—but with that one comment, I ruined the relationship she had with that horse for the next 10 years. It was unsettling to realize how much influence I had on her and how easily a passing comment can become a passing blow. I took the lesson to heart and have measured my words more carefully since. Especially when a topic is controversial, I keep my opinions to myself as much as possible. Rather than espousing my views on immigration, capital punishment, oil exploration, or political candidates, for instance, I prefer to take a Socratic approach. Before they broach a heated topic, I let them know that I will participate only by posing questions to further dialogue among them. In this way, I help them look at an issue deeply and from a variety of vantage points, but I let them draw their own conclusions on topics rather than give them mine. This also has the convenient side benefit of setting a precedent for not commenting when they push the student-teacher boundary into my personal life. Having already established the ground rules, my choosing not to answer questions that are none of their business does not automatically confirm their suspicions.

Does this standing back mean that a teacher should be devoid of personality? Certainly not. Passion for the subject, a sense of humor, and genuine interest in the students are invaluable to learning. Without a warm personality that makes the kids feel safe to ask questions and make mistakes, the classroom echoes with awkward, shallow hollowness. Do I tell stories to my students? Sure. Lots of them. After all, language is the medium of the storyteller. It's very appropriate that I use my experiences to prompt them to write about theirs. I remember, though, that they are the stars of the show and that developing their ideas is more important than promoting my own. I am the director, and when things go well, I turn that role over to them, too, and slip into the background as a supporting character.

What I need to remember is that the podium is not a pulpit. These are my students; they are not my congregation. It is my job to expand their minds, not to narrow them. It is not right for me to try to make my causes be their causes. I teach my students to do research but am careful about telling them what to research. Of course, I have parameters, but I let the area of study, rather than my view of the world, set those limits. My students research controversial issues like mutilation as a rite of passage, reintroduction of wolves, contemporary slave trade, and the existence of miracles. I encourage them to read widely when researching and to use credible sources. I don't use this as an opportunity to gain converts to my way of thinking by steering them only toward authors who support my philosophies. And, if students want to investigate topics that are pretty edgy, I solicit the parents' approval. For instance, one student, in researching vampires, wanted to join a chat room for people who feel they are vampires. I turned that over to her parents; that decision was too big for me to make. If I can accidentally make one girl hate her horse, I sure don't want to influence another's thirst for blood. I just want her to know how to research and report her findings.

Again, keeping objectives broad is the surest way of excluding a teacher's biases from the curriculum. This is most easily done by prescribing the skill to be learned rather than the topic. That's the point of differentiated instruction. It's not meant to be a way for students who hate writing to avoid it by instead sketching scenes from a story. If the skill to be demonstrated by the student is summarizing, then sure, the picture route is valid. But if the skill being taught is writing, let the students have a say in what they write. Nothing promotes commitment to a project more than genuine interest in the subject matter.

Of course, learning has to be done within a context. I have to use books to teach reading. I have to talk so they learn to listen. They have to have a prompt to focus their writing. But choosing the context has to be done with the students, not me, in mind. It is right to select quality literature so they can see examples of excellent writing. It is great to pick a wide variety of sources so they are exposed to different ways of looking at the world.

A teacher was once telling me about how his semester had gone. Among his list of proudest accomplishments was finally, *finally*, getting a boy to look at a piece of literature from a perspective that wasn't Christian. All I could wonder was how long it had taken that boy's parents to get him to see everything from a Christian point of view, from their perspective. Though the teacher felt he had done the student a great service by widening his horizons, he had, in fact, overstepped his claim to that boy.

The danger for a teacher comes when she teaches too personally, especially in accordance with her own agenda. A teacher cannot forget, as I did with that first class, that these are not her own children. They have been entrusted to us by their parents to educate, not to indoctrinate. I am not entitled to make them junior versions of me. We are hired by their parents; we are accountable to them. And when we return their children to them, we should have increased their ability to learn, widened their horizons, not narrowed their focus to ours.

There have been times when I have taught literature that I thought some parents might find objectionable. One semester, for instance, as part of the Montana Heritage Project, my students collected oral histories from Vietnam War veterans. It was important for the students to have some background on this controversial war before they met with the veterans. Toward that end, I wanted them to read Tim O'Brien's (1990) *The Things They Carried*. It is a great piece of literature, and it presents a variety of perspectives on the war. It has some graphic violence, however, and plenty of coarse language; I had reservations about teaching the book myself. So I opted to let the parents decide whether they wanted their children to read it. I sent home a letter describing the book. I let the parents know that I felt the violence and language were not gratuitous but essential to the story. As O'Brien himself said in the introduction to the book, "Send guys to war, they come home talking dirty" (69). I told them that I felt the book certainly had enough redeeming social value to warrant the harshness, and I offered to lend a copy to anyone who wanted to preview it.

Some parents couldn't believe I was asking for permission; one borrowed a copy, not because he was concerned, but because he was intrigued; the majority agreed to let their children read it; and two sets of parents said they did not want their kids to read the book. I was fine with that. There were plenty of other books for them to read. So, while the rest of us read O'Brien's book, these two students did independent studies. One researched the history of the Vietnamese conflict, and the other read Studs Terkel's *The Good War* to learn about conducting oral interviews. They presented their research to the rest of the class, and our understanding of the project was broadened because of their parents' direction. And again, that's the value of differentiated instruction.

The family of one of the aforementioned students is Baptist. The other is Mormon. There are plenty of both in this town. I also teach many Catholics, Lutherans, and Evangelical Christians. I have had a student who was raised on a Hutterite colony. Our community of 700 has its own Mennonite school with over 50 students. Our town is surrounded by thousands of acres of barley. Suffice it to say, it's a pretty conservative place. I knew that when I moved here. I knew it when I decided to teach here. And since they, as taxpayers, are my employers, I feel it is only right to respect their values.

I met a woman at an Advanced Placement conference who was from a large city in the East. She was telling me about some of the controversial novels she teaches, and I asked whether she informs parents before teaching them. She was clearly taken aback and said she certainly did not. The parents of her students, she said, expect that she will have free rein with regard to what they study when their children enter her class. I told her about the conservative demographics of our town and her eyes went wide. Well, maybe then, she said, and walked away.

To her, parental oversight sounded down-home and sheltered, and it is, but those are considered positive attributes in a rural school. Rural parents like their kids to be *their* kids. So, innocuous or noble as my intentions may be, I need to be cautious about where I tread. I admit that I cannot always resist the temptation to voice my opinion or to smile widest at the student whose belief concurs with my own. But at least I try to be aware when I do it. That's probably as honest an approach as can be expected.

References

Barkley, C. (1993). Nike Air commercial. Retrieved on June 26, 2014, from http:// youtube/nMzdAZ3TjCA.

Bloom, B.S. (1956). *Taxonomy of educational objectives, handbook I: The cognitive domain.* New York, NY: David McKay Co. Inc.

O'Brien, T. (1990). *The things they carried.* New York, NY: Broadway Books.

11

TEACHING AND LEARNING AT NAY AH SHING SCHOOL

Gregg Rutter, Roger Nieboer, Govinda Budrow, and Bambi O' Hern

NAY AH SHING SCHOOL, MILLE LACS BAND OF OJIBWE RESERVATION, ONAMIA, MINNESOTA

Nay Ah Shing Tribal School is located on the Mille Lacs Band of Ojibwe Reservation in central Minnesota. The school began in 1975 as a result of community and tribal leaders' vision and desire to provide educational services for the reservation children. There was significant prejudice against Native Americans at the public school in the area that eventually led to a school walk out by Mille Lacs Band students; this event was a primary catalyst in starting Nay Ah Shing School.

Today the school sits on beautiful property near the Mille Lacs Band Government Center, clinic, health and human services facility, and just down the road from the History Museum and Trading Post. Nay Ah Shing School is a very small K-12 school with a student body of approximately just 200. The school consists of two buildings, 'Abinoojiiyag' elementary (K–5) and the upper school (6–12). A wonderful area with a natural pathway winds through oak trees and passes by an outdoor classroom; this pathway connects the two school buildings. The outdoor classroom is used for cultural activities that include boiling maple sap in the spring and preparing wild rice in the fall.

Nay Ah Shing is a BIE (Bureau of Indian Education) school. We not only teach to the academic standards of Minnesota but we also focus on teaching and honoring traditional Ojibwe culture. Twice a month we begin the school day with a traditional pipe ceremony. In the fall we organize opportunities for gathering wild rice and in the spring students participate in tapping maple trees and making syrup. The school's curriculum includes Ojibwe language and Ojibwe culture classes. There is a generational gap of Ojibwe language speakers due in part to the past Indian boarding schools' practice of only allowing English to be used; now there is a concerted effort to reestablish Ojibwe language, recognizing that language is a critical aspect of maintaining a culture.

★★★

As I was completing my teaching degree, vivid dreams colored my nights. Dreams of being surrounded by children as we looked through a window at the impending storm rolling toward us. We talk in Ojibwe, noticing the colors of the storm clouds in beautiful shades of purple and pinks. Another night begins with a dark classroom as I am piercing the poles for a wigwam into the tiled classroom floor. It takes many attempts as the floor cracks to reveal the earth beneath, allowing the poles to settle into the intended position. These dreams positioned my teaching over a decade ago as I applied to teach at a rural tribal school. The dreams reminded me that a fusion of our traditional ways and the classroom was needed. This path to blending these worlds has been rocky, lacking in simplicity and full of duality.

During my first year of teaching, I tried to encourage students to sound out phonetic words and found out very quickly that I was hitting a language barrier that I should have been anticipating. The children understood phonics but they also understood the types of acceptable speech patterns in 'Indian country.' The word 'pants' was the downfall of my sound-it-out plan. All my first grade students confidently wrote the word pants as P-A-N-T-I-S. Then I heard it clear as day, my mother and grandmother talking about the new 'pant-is' and making sure they had their 'pant-is' packed. My mind rustled with the crisp sounds of these words. This was not a phonics issue as much as the fact that I neglected to recognize the script we were raised within and that I needed to pull out that script and use it in my teaching. This fusion of worlds again bumping on the path of conflicting duality.

Some may argue that students need to know it is wrong to say 'pantis' and in some ways I would agree. Pantis, however, has spanned at least two generations for me, and for my first graders I am sure a solid three generations. I don't pretend to understand where it came from but I do know that it exists in a way that has crossed generations and tribal affiliations. Historically, the loss of traditional culture, language, and parenting through outlawing traditional ceremonies, mandating boarding schools, and relocation devastated tribal communities. I chose affirmation and looked at it no differently than the dream of pointing out the colors of the storm approaching. I explained how we hear the word pants as pantis in our communities and that in books and many other communities we will hear pants. We learned the correct way to spell pantis as P-A-N-T-S. We understood that our feet were planted firmly on the ground, one foot in both worlds with solid fusion holding on to our pantis because this ride between bridging worlds was far from over.

★★★

One of the challenges of learning and teaching at Nay Ah Shing is student attendance. From kindergarten through the twelfth grade, student attendance is an issue. The reason students miss school reflects both a low SES profile and an apparent lack of emphasis on the importance of education within some of the families. Some students miss the school bus and then have no way to get to school because the family doesn't have a car or because the parent/guardian is at work or still sleeping after working late. Some students miss school because they are home taking care of younger siblings; others miss school because they have been up all night for a variety of reasons. Older students may simply make the choice on their own that they won't go to school, and, unfortunately, there is not a responsible adult in their life who can insist they attend school.

Some students are habitually late to school. One teacher relayed the incident of a student who arrived at school with only one hour left in the day. When she asked why he was so late, he simply said that he needed to help clean the house. She explained to him that his job was to be at school, to which he replied, "My sister has scabies, we had to wash everything in hot bleach water and wipe everything down." Other students are late because of chronic lice problems and they can't get a good night's sleep.

These persistent attendance issues, of course, have a serious detrimental effect on the individual student's learning; however, this issue also causes a tremendous teaching challenge. It is imperative that teachers at Nay Ah Shing are flexible with their lesson plans and are able to adapt to change. Students may also miss school for cultural activities such as going to Pow Wows or fishing and hunting. Teachers have to use these opportunities advantageously, be it differentiating instruction with small group learning or building on student experiences to connect content with meaningful life experiences.

To encourage good attendance, the school provides quarterly awards for perfect and near-perfect attendance. This system, though, emphasizes external motivation and does not take into account legitimate excuses for being absent. The attendance issue continues to be an area of concern and an area that presents an opportunity for improvement.

★★★

The Pow Wow is scheduled to start in the high school gym at 10 A.M.

At 9:30 A.M. students are released from class to change into dance regalia and assist with Pow Wow preparations.

At 9:45 A.M. the IT guy begins setting up the PA system, a few tribal elders chat in one corner of the gym, and the smell of popping popcorn wafts in from the hall.

At 10 A.M. students and community members begin trickling into the gym, a few drummers start setting up small circles of chairs around the drums, and the MC tests the microphone.

At 10:15 A.M. people start flowing into the gym, the MC announces that the Grand Entry is about to begin and that all dancers should line up in the hallway. Excitement and anticipation build as the drummers begin to warm up.

At 10:20 A.M. the MC asks for any military veterans in the crowd to please come forward to serve as flag bearers for the Grand Entry.

At 10:25 A.M. there is a roll call of the drums and the MC determines that there are two full drum groups in attendance.

At 10:30 A.M. the MC asks if anyone knows the whereabouts of the flags (the US Stars and Stripes, as well as the powder blue flag of the tribal government, have apparently gone missing). Somebody tells the MC that the missing flags must be down in the elementary school; he sends someone down there to get the flags, and then makes a few jokes about forgetfulness.

At 10:40 A.M. the missing flags, now found, are handed to the military honor guard. The MC instructs the Host Drum to begin the first honor song, and with the pounding of the drum, the Pow Wow begins.

To a rookie, non-Native teacher, it might very well have seemed that the Pow Wow just started 40 minutes late, amidst chaotic circumstances that could clearly have been avoided with more thorough and rigorous planning and preparation.

To someone who has spent any time in a reservation school, that Pow Wow went off without a hitch. Yeah, there was that little holdup about the missing flags, but hey, they found them, didn't they? And the popcorn was really good. And the kids danced beautifully, and people from the community had a really good time.

A non-Native teacher working in a reservation school faces many challenges, the most intriguing of which may be processing the concept of 'Indian Time.' We quickly learn how to talk about it, joke about it, laugh about it, and maybe, eventually, appreciate and embrace it.

Many schools, by their very nature, depend upon timekeeping and punctuality to provide structure and coherence to their insular sanctum of learning. They often form distinct committees specifically devoted to creating academic calendars, class schedules, and daily planners.

As teachers, we learn to work in strict accordance with that school calendar, dividing it precisely into semesters, quarters, weeks, days, blocks, hours, periods, and minutes. Within these parameters, we strive to develop challenging academic goals for our students, devise appropriate learning strategies, and create data-driven lesson plans. We have been trained to manage time effectively and efficiently, with the assistance of clocks and timers and buzzers and bells.

Our conventional school day, perhaps the ultimate human construct, developed in close philosophical and sociological alliance with the all-American, 8-hour work day and 40-hour week. There is nothing natural about it. In the winter, we arrive and depart in darkness. In late spring and early fall there is plenty of daylight to make it all the way to school and home again.

As we gaze out our classroom windows at bald eagles soaring majestically over a 33,000-acre lake the color of the sky, any constraint brought about by an arbitrary measure of time can begin to seem brazenly absurd. We are surrounded by a natural world of immense proportions and profound beauty.

Perhaps we can begin to understand how a concept of time, radically different from that responsible for the implementation of the conventional school day, might have developed here. This concept, born of the need to survive in a harsh environment, and totally dependent on the bountifulness of nature, concerned itself more with the daily rhythms of life, the rising and setting of the sun, the cycles of the moon, and the changing of the seasons.

***

Nay Ah Shing is a very small school. Class sizes are small and there are only one or two grade-level classes. There are Ojibwe language teachers, Ojibwe culture teachers, a Physical Education teacher at each school, an art teacher, and a gifted and talented education teacher. We do not have a music department, a band or choir, or football, baseball, or hockey teams. We do have committed professional educators who work hard, do what is best for children, and generously help one another out. Sometimes this means bringing in a new pair of shoes, boots, pants, or jacket for a child. It means keeping snacks handy for those students who don't get enough to eat outside of school. It means making sure students who want to read a book, have a book to read outside of school. It means knowing a student's life outside of school so the right accommodations can be made for that student to feel safe and successful. It means giving kids a consistent, stable environment. And it means maintaining high expectations for student learning.

Because we are in a rural area, there are extremely limited numbers of substitute, or guest, teachers available. When a teacher is absent there may not be a substitute teacher to fill that spot, so the rest of the staff pulls together and makes it work. There are also limited outside professional development opportunities. Sometimes we travel 100 miles or more to participate in professional development workshops. At the same time, because the school is so small, teachers have the chance for their voices and ideas to be heard, and to be engaged in many aspects of the school. Being a tribal school, all staff has the chance to get involved with the community in many ways. Participating in and showing up at Mille Lacs Band events is so important in building connections and creating engagement between the school and the broader tribal community.

***

Culture creates meaning and teaching fashions humility. One of the characteristics of working in a small rural school is that your job description is flexible and it is not unusual to move from grade to grade to teach where you are needed. I was teaching fourth grade and working on state reports with the students. The students were creating PowerPoint presentations on the state that they were studying. They had to research topics like state flags, birds, characteristics, and capitals. We went over topics and added them to our reports with text and pictures. I was checking over the day's progress on state seals and noticed one student wrote a wonderfully descriptive paragraph about the seal for her state and included a picture of a large, grey, whiskery seal. I giggled as I thought about the perception the student must have had about what I was explaining and I knew that I had to work harder to create a meaning for these new words.

Meaning can be skewed in other ways as well. Each year a favorite story in our reading series is a simple beginning reading book, *The Cow That Went Moo*. The story is about a cow that travels through several situations going moo. To students in other rural communities, or even students in suburban and urban communities, this story might be common and bland. At our school this story elicits wide-eyed smiles from our youngest readers that quickly break into belly-jiggling giggles. The culture and language constructs of this story transform it from one of a cow making sounds in different places, to a cow in a much-altered context. The ability to understand is tied to the meaning of the Ojibwe word *moo*, which is translated to English as poop. I will give you a moment for your cultural context to embrace the story, *The Cow That Went Moo*. It is actually a difficult set of stories to get through with teachers and students laughing. Unlike pantis, *The Cow That Went Moo* does not get an explicit lesson. It has become a silent cultural test of whether or not you get the meaning of this story. It is our giggly, twinkling eye story that connects us to each other and crosses these worlds through our laughter.

★★★

It is a small community. Sometimes it seems like everybody is related to everybody else. There is also a larger, more extended community; students might have close relatives who live on another reservation or live in Minneapolis. Students might live with a grandparent or auntie or uncle, then later move and live with a parent or stepparent, or they might live in a foster home. There is a considerable amount of illicit drug use, and a considerable number of parents in prison or somehow in the court system. It seems that most, if not all, the students know someone close to them that has died a tragic death.

Drug abuse is a very serious problem on the reservation. Students are exposed to alcohol, marijuana, methamphetamine, cocaine, heroin, and prescription drugs at such an early age that they don't recognize it as out of the ordinary, which for them it isn't. Not only are some students' parents or other family members in jail or prison for drug-related issues, it is not uncommon to know of a family member who died of a drug overdose. The expectation that a parent who has been to jail will go back to jail is high among our kids, so it becomes commonplace. The children are used to such tragedy and are not surprised by much.

★★★

While there are certainly sad stories and tragedies beyond the norm in the lives of our students, there is also a deep sense of caring, community, and unconditional love. There are many intact families as well on the reservation. There is a strong desire and commitment to honor, protect, and preserve a rich and admirable culture. There is a wanting and need for an education that enables these students to be successful in two cultures, and develop skills they can use to improve lives on the reservation. It is the job of teachers at Nay Ah Shing to provide the opportunities that will promote engagement and meaning to student learning within the twenty-first-century Ojibwe community.

When I first started teaching at Nay Ah Shing I was told that if I made it through the first year I would never leave. I know why; it is the incredible connection with students, connection with families, and becoming a part of a truly loving and caring community of people who have a deep regard and respect for their past and a vision for their future, that make me never want to leave.

★★★

What exactly is 'Indian Time'?

It's a tough concept for an outsider to grasp, and even more difficult to explain. I once naïvely asked a respected tribal elder/spiritual leader to define 'Indian Time.' He looked at me with a pained expression on his face, shrugged his shoulders, and chuckled softly while shaking his head. "Things happen when they are supposed to happen." End of conversation.

Some non-Native teachers initially and erroneously think of 'Indian Time' as being synonymous with 'running late.' Be forewarned: 'Indian Time' refers to a complex conceptual time construct that differs from conventional school time in several subtle and highly nuanced ways. 'Indian Time' might just as well refer to occasions of 'starting early,' particularly when involving activities related to hunting, fishing, or gathering of natural crops.

"When the maple sap starts running, we basically have to drop everything and go to the sugar bush to collect the sap," explains our tribal high school's biology teacher. "We try to plan it out in advance, as to when it is most likely to happen. But every year it's different. It all depends on the weather, and how the weather affects the trees."

"Nature rules. We're at the whims of our environment. We never know exactly when it will happen, until it happens," adds our cultural coordinator. "And when it happens, we have to respond. It's a limited window of opportunity."

Within a classroom setting, of course, this uncertainty can be highly unsettling and disruptive, and for new teachers, highly frustrating as well. "It drove me crazy, my first couple of years here," a non-Native colleague explains. "But then I learned to just go with it. Seriously, flexibility is the key. Be prepared, and be prepared to improvise. That's become my motto."

The whole notion of 'planning,' which is so pervasive in the minds of many teachers, might be looked upon as ludicrous by some traditional tribal elders, who have on occasion expressed the belief that planning for anything more than four days in advance is not only preposterous, but might actually be construed as an insult to Gichi Manidoo (Great Spirit). Some of these elders feel that long-range planning is a waste of time, a presumptuous human foible flying in the face of destinies influenced by spiritual forces beyond our imagination and control.

"It's not so much that we are forbidden to plan, or that we shouldn't plan, but that we recognize the limitations, that we recognize the transitory nature of the universe," explained one Native teacher. "We are always encouraged to dream of the future, to imagine the possibilities. So if and when we do plan, we do so with the understanding that everything might change . . . suddenly and unexpectedly. We try to live in the moment, and not become locked in to any rigid, preconceived master plan."

This philosophy permeates traditional beliefs and often trickles down to even the youngest children. For a classroom teacher, that can present a unique series of challenges in dealing with students and academic expectations. Everything from developing an outline for a writing project to forming long-range career goals can be impacted by this underlying cultural ideal.

"Kids are very perceptive," observes one veteran English teacher. "They pick up on even the tiniest hint of cultural incongruity. And are often quick to point out, 'That's not how we do things.' I usually deal with it by falling back on our school's mission statement, which states very clearly that our goal is to provide kids with the skills to live in two worlds. Of course, that isn't easy. It's always a balancing act. But if you can address it head on, you can avoid a lot of potential misunderstanding, and hopefully, inspire the kids to think seriously about some really important issues that they will continue to face for the rest of their lives."

By 1 P.M., many of the younger kids at the Pow Wow are getting tired and cranky. Their teachers can readily sense when the kids have had enough. The original plan is for all students to stay at the Pow Wow until 3 P.M., but the kindergarten and first grade teachers make the collective decision to head back to their classrooms early. In a more restrictive environment, that violation of protocol might become an issue. Here, no one questions their decision; everybody understands.

★★★

Part of bridging worlds is embracing time as a conceptual context and a cultural philosophy. The running joke about 'Indian Time' as a construct of Native people showing up late or starting events well past the scheduled time is really misconstrued. Some people will take offense to the idea of 'Indian Time' existing, despite the multitude of examples of things and people seemingly running behind schedule. This perception is misunderstood as a matter of lateness or a state of being behind schedule, when in reality it is about accepting where you are supposed to be within any given moment. 'Indian Time' rejects the fear of future and willingly takes in the moment. It is present in the acceptance of things happening for a reason and lessons coming together at the right time. It is not about being late as much as it is about being present in the now.

This concept of time is reflected in indigenous teaching practices and it has come to struggle in how we bond this modern gap between worlds. One student really exemplified this struggle when he came to my classroom as a first grader. This student's kindergarten year was spent one-on-one with a special education teacher. That year, they wanted to have him join the classroom. He was nearly nonverbal with the exception of some hard to understand swear words that he would scream at the class as he hoped to leave to go back to the comfort of his known, isolated classroom. We worked through each day and eventually he accepted the class as his own. His language skills were rapidly developing being around peers and the constant communication in the classroom. The students were patient and supportive.

The struggle came to a head as curriculum decisions were being decided for this student. Professionals trying to project into his future potential were looking at this child and noting life skills as more important and that his probability of learning to read was limited. I looked at this seven-year-old that was clearly on his own time schedule and thought, who can really predict his potential; I didn't feel comfortable with this imposed future prognosis limiting his access to curriculum. I advocated that we stay in this moment and test the true extent of his potential by teaching him to read. The only way to know how far one can go is to allow them to begin the journey. This student stayed in my class over the course of three years and I was able to watch him develop moment after moment.

At the end of third grade, I reflected on this amazing child. He was reading, doing math, communicating, and he had friendships. He had come so far, but all within his own time frame. We were all proud. That pride was quickly marred by the outlook of our standardized testing for the state. The state rates children between three stages: does not meet standards, meets standards, and exceeds standards. Despite the major leaps and bounds this student had achieved, we were all too aware that the progress wasn't going to register positively on the state scale. The state at the time allowed schools to exempt 1 percent of the students from taking the standard test based on disabilities, but we were a rural school with less than 100 kids taking the test. We had no 1 percent to turn to and he had to take that test. I remember the heaviness of that day, giving a test to a boy that was working on 'Indian Time' and was going to be judged on mainstream, literal time. Not only judged but also deemed as not meeting up to this imposed standard.

We have to find ways to shake off imposed standards and celebrate our own truths; there is so much to be celebrated.

Bibliography for Further Reading

Alexie, S. (2007). *The absolutely true diary of a part-time Indian.* New York, NY: Little, Brown and Company.
Bergstrom, A., Cleary, L. M., & Peacock, T. D. (2003). *The seventh generation: Native students speak about finding the good path.* Charleston, WV: ERIC Clearinghouse on Rural Education and Small Schools.

Cleary, L. M., & Peacock, T. D. (1998). *Collected wisdom: American Indian education.* Boston, MA: Allyn and Bacon.

Kalyanpur, M., & Harry, B. (2012). *Cultural reciprocity in special education: Building family-professional relationships.* Baltimore, MD: Paul H. Brookes Publishing Co.

Kegg, M. (1993). *Portage lake: Memories of an Ojibwe childhood.* Minneapolis, MN: University of Minnesota Press.

Nabakov, P. (Ed.) (1999). *Native American testimony: A chronicle of Indian-white relations from prophecy to the present, 1492–2000* (Rev. ed.). E. Rutherford, NJ: Penguin Books.

12

TEACHING IN MY OWN VOICE: A 30-YEAR PEDAGOGICAL JOURNEY

Sharon Bishop

HEARTLAND COMMUNITY SCHOOL, HENDERSON, NEBRASKA

ENGAGING VOICE: In the best writing, you can hear the writer's voice—his or her special way of expressing ideas and emotions.

(Sebranek, Kemper, and Meyer, 2001)

Introduction

I sat in the lovely room at the St. Benedict's Center, part of a professional writing retreat sponsored by the Nebraska Writing Project, with a young man and a young woman, both teachers with less experience than I—but I felt as if I had been demoted. Both of my companions were teachers in a large metropolitan school district while I had taught in a small, rural school for almost 30 years. Teaching in the larger city and district were clearly superior to the young woman, who was dismissive of my experience in the same place for so long; I had not met her definition of moving up on the academic ladder. Her unspoken message was that if I were a really good teacher, I would have left that tiny school behind long ago. Our task that day was to share our curricula from our schools. My fellow teachers shared their spreadsheets on their laptops, lesson plans for a whole year that had been constructed, for the most part, by someone else, perhaps the 'curriculum coordinators' in that district. This spread sheet reflected a typical literature class with attendant writing assignments. When I looked more closely at the sheet in front of me, I noticed that there was a timeline given for teaching each assignment; for example, teaching *Romeo and Juliet* was to take three weeks. I asked, "What happens if you can't get it done in three weeks?" The answer: a shrug and a terse reply—"No choice!"

I thought of all of the latitude I'd been given in my small, rural school. My Language Arts curriculum, secondary English and Speech, had been chosen and constructed, for the most part, by me. And there was a great deal of latitude in the creation of that student work. Although I often used anthologies, I could depart from them when I chose to. When the fiftieth anniversary of the Blizzard of 1949 rolled around, my students collected stories from family and community members about their memories of that event. When a local artist constructed a sculpture depicting early irrigation methods in the 1950s, my students spent much of that school year interviewing farmers and farm wives as well as now adult children who remembered when the coming of irrigation changed the lives of agriculture and the community. A state-wide commemoration of the building of Interstate 80, which runs just three miles north of town, motivated my students to imagine a landscape without the four lanes of concrete and to conduct interviews with community elders who recalled that time, providing a connection of the local with a national event. The year before our school consolidation officially took place, my students studied how an earlier merger in the early 1950s had also brought stress to the community when the small neighborhood 'country schools' were disbanded and all students came to town to learn. How could I possibly ever teach in a school that did not allow me to juggle the curriculum so that these kinds of assignments could become an integral part of learning? Still, the reaction of this young teacher was one I had encountered before. Colleagues would often urge me to find a job in a larger school, the implication clearly being that there was more prestige in such jobs. The salary would have been better, but I was always held in check by the dread that I would not have the freedom to create the work in my own classroom, that my teaching voice would be lost in the impersonal spreadsheets that someone else had designed.

I stepped into 'my' classroom for the first time in August 1979. I had just signed a contract to teach Secondary Language Arts in a small rural school in eastern Nebraska. My earlier teaching experience had been in a larger town and school in Kansas and this small town would be a different experience for me even though I had attended grades K–12 in one town in another part of Nebraska. This new town, however, was the smallest place I had ever lived, population 999, as the sign proudly proclaimed on the outskirts of a neat village that had cornfields growing right up to the edge of the city limits. I had interviewed with the superintendent in Lincoln, the capital city, at the University of Nebraska where I had been taking postgraduate classes. The superintendent told me that the town he represented, Henderson, had a Mennonite history and was a farm community; he stressed that this was a 'modern Mennonite' community with a proud heritage and a progressive present. When I drove the hour west of Lincoln to meet him and to tour the town and school, I found that his pride in his hometown seemed justified: The houses and yards were clean and neat, the Main Street held a variety of small businesses, and two city parks and a swimming pool hosted active, laughing children. In addition to the fields of corn and soybeans, a large elevator and several agribusinesses dealing with irrigation were prominent. In fact, the elevator was adjacent to the school's parking lot. Little did I know then that the sound of that elevator would become a kind of 'white noise' background for my life for the next 32 years. Although I had expected to stay in this place at this job for two to three years, I ended up teaching in that same classroom for over three decades, teaching students whose parents I'd taught a generation before. One of the reasons that I stayed beyond that projected short time frame was the latitude I was given by the administration to create much of the curricula that I used to teach classes in secondary Speech and English. Much would change over those three decades: small farms would disappear and more of my students lived in town; declining enrollment meant a merger with an adjoining town and a new name for the resultant consolidated school; technology would find its way into our school and classrooms; and state standards and assessments created a new vocabulary for teachers and administrators. Our school would become part of a nationwide initiative in the late 1990s and early 2000s that focused on the value of rural schools, and I and several of my colleagues would become affiliated with the Nebraska Writing Project. Throughout all of these changes, there was one factor that remained almost constant: I was given the freedom to create the curricula for my classes. Although it was not always a smooth journey, this freedom became so important to me that I could not envision teaching anywhere else. This chapter will describe the opportunities, issues, and some of the obstacles of teaching in this one place.

A Beginning

The initial visit to my classroom showed me a space much like the one I'd sat in for the four years of my own high school experience: a teacher's desk at the front of the room with a green blackboard as backdrop, and student desks arranged in neat rows. The 1950s architecture of the building was still present, with glass blocks arranged above the windows; a pencil sharpener was bolted to the wooden bookshelves beneath the windows and the shelves held dictionaries and other assorted books. I was most interested in examining these textbooks. A visit with the secondary principal had given me the somewhat distressing news that the previous teacher had left no curriculum guides behind. The principal had merely given me a list of the classes that I would teach: seventh grade Speech, eighth grade Reading, sophomore English, high school Speech, and senior English. The superintendent had made it clear to me in the first interview that almost 100 percent of the graduating seniors attended some kind of post-secondary educational institution and that I was to make sure that my students were ready for this academic work beyond high school. I began a search for textbooks. There was an older anthology for sophomore English, a British Literature book for seniors, but there were no textbooks for the Speech classes. I later learned from an aide that the reading class consisted of individual packets whose masters were stored in file cabinets in the elementary wing of the school; I was to mimeograph these packets for the students, who were all in different lessons. I was most concerned with the Speech curriculum; I had not taught Speech before but had confidently told the superintendent in the first interview that I could easily teach those classes.

Putting together the sophomore and senior English classes was the easiest as I had taught English previously and this was what I had been prepared to teach. I immediately added a heavy component of writing to these classes, particularly in the senior classes. Students read literature and wrote long, in-depth analyses of this literature; to prepare for research assignments in college, students chose a novel to read and I set up a visit to the University of Nebraska's Love Library to research literary backgrounds of the novels that students had read. When we entered the doors of this large building, the kids' eyes grew big and a bit apprehensive but with help from the staff, they soon learned how to use the card catalog and to disappear into the stacks of books and emerge with armfuls of college-level reading to load onto the bus and take back home for use. The 'big senior paper'—a tradition that would last for 32 years—had begun. Within one year, I began to receive feedback from that first class of seniors who had gone on to colleges: some to Mennonite colleges in Kansas, some to the University and other smaller colleges and universities, some to the technical classes in the state's community colleges system. They reported that they had been prepared to write well. One young man told me a story of how he had turned in a paper in an agricultural class at the University of Kansas; his instructor had called him in and grilled him, not believing that a college freshman could write so well. These stories would repeat themselves over and over for the next three decades. This early success ensured that I would have administrative and community support for the writing strand of my English classes.

Creating a curriculum for the Speech classes was a bit more difficult. I racked my brain for topics for speeches and, quite honestly, learned how to teach Speech as I went along. Soon, I was hearing the same kind of feedback from kids who went away to college: They were more prepared to write and deliver a speech than many of their contemporaries. I learned how to construct a junior high speech class that would prepare students for the high school class. That first Fall I was also asked to sponsor a competitive Speech Team and again, I learned more from the seniors than they learned from me! But soon, the Speech Team was qualifying participants for State competition and the team won several Conference and District awards.

After struggling with a mass of individual reading packets for one year, I asked my principal if I could purchase paperback novels for the junior high reading class and teach them all at the same time. He agreed and I felt more in control of what I was teaching. Eventually, that class would be removed because of scheduling problems. By now I was feeling very confident as a teacher of these diverse Language Arts classes and I felt that I could make decisions about the choices of literary selections and writing assignments. I was, however, always mindful of the moral environment of the community. Despite a religious and somewhat conservative history, the community was not intrusive. There were a few occasions when parents questioned my choice of a book but the school district had in place a policy for these occasions; only once in 32 years did I have a parent take a book to a committee. A group of teachers and citizens upheld the right of the novel to remain on a list of book choices.

Constructing a Curriculum of Place

One of the earliest observations I made about this community was the strong sense of local history. When I asked my first classes to describe this place to me they could tell me of the ethnic foods brought by the Germans from Russia who had first settled here in 1887, leaving Russia for the freedom to practice the Mennonite belief of pacifism. Most of them knew this early history and they were proud of the farming traditions within their families. Several generations of families still gathered for Sunday and holiday family dinners and many of the students identified their relationship with fellow students by the degree of those relatives; "He is my third cousin" and "We are second cousins." I understood that there was a rich tradition here to be tapped by students and I assigned oral history interviews and writing assignments that reflected family stories and customs. Somehow, these assignments were blended into a more traditional study of literature in the sophomore and senior classes.

Then, about two years into my teaching career, I asked my sophomore students if they were familiar with Nebraska authors and their works. Despite being a low population state, Nebraska has a proud and productive literary history. The most well-known is Willa Cather whose work is found in most American literature anthologies. There are other writers as well: John Neihardt, Bess Streeter Aldrich, Mari Sandoz, Loren Eiseley, and Wright Morris. Many contemporary poets were publishing as well including Ted Kooser, who would be named Poet Laureate of the United States in 2004; Bill Kloefkorn who was the official state poet of Nebraska for 30 years; Don Welch, Marjorie Saiser, Twyla Hansen, and others who wrote specifically about this place and these people. It seemed to me that to live in a place and not know this literary history left a huge gap in students' educations. Over the summer I prepared a curriculum that would introduce these writers into the sophomore English class. To make sure that I would cover all of the necessary skills in this class, I called the Language Arts consultant at the Nebraska State Department of Education. He reminded me that Nebraska did not have any specific State Standards for the teaching of English and that we still relied on 'local control' in our state; although I knew this, I wanted to make sure my new class contained sufficient rigor. He simply wished me good luck and told me that I only had to convince my local board of education. Both the secondary principal and the superintendent approved of my new sophomore English class and submitted my written proposal to the board of education, who approved it. I hedged my bets a bit by still retaining the traditional anthology for some of the work and by still calling the class Sophomore English.

Gradually, however, I began to use the traditional anthology less and less and then discarded it completely for a class that I called 'Nebraska Literature &

Composition: A Sense of Place.' In addition to the usual activities that accompany any study of literature, I expanded the use of local and regional history. A preserved prairie a few miles from our school became available as an 'outdoor classroom' and soon the Biology teacher, who shared the same students who were in sophomore English, and I began to teach a parallel unit and we took the students together to the prairie in the Fall to sit under the clear blue sky and observe and write and experience this ecosystem that is the foundation of our lives here on the Plains. For the Biology class, students collected plant specimens and identified the native grasses. I also asked students to take a camera along; part of their English assignment would be to observe closely and find the unexpected, the beauty of a prairie that seemed at first glance to them just a piece of abandoned pasture browning in the September sun. Their rural backgrounds had shaped their thinking about the land, useful for growing corn and soybeans, the crops that surrounded this plot of 50 acres of preserved prairie. The writing in their reflective journals showed a connection with this prairie, historically and aesthetically.

One of the novels I chose for this class was by a University of Nebraska professor who wrote about the Sand Hill cranes and their migration. This natural phenomenon was quickly becoming a large tourist draw for the central part of Nebraska. Each year, in February and March, thousands and thousands of the large Sand Hill cranes stop in the Platte River Valley as they migrate north to nesting grounds in Siberia and the Arctic Circle. The Platte, a prairie river, is ideally suited to these birds who roost in its shallow waters and feed in the adjacent wet meadows and cornfields. The 5–6 week stopover is crucial to the birds: They must gain enough weight to fly north and build a nest many, many miles away. A dammed and diverted Platte River has reduced the flyway to about 80 miles and now tourists flocked to see the dramatic spectacle of these birds. It seemed clear that another outdoor classroom had been discovered, although this one was not as close as the prairie. The Biology teacher and I submitted the cost of the field trip in both of our budgets and this was approved by the administration. Another tradition had begun, 'the crane trip.'

Other outdoor classrooms included trips to regional museums and each request was again approved by the administration. Combining Biology and English for many of these trips meant a richer curriculum for the students. The writing and photography done on site became essays and poetry of place and these were put into a class-made book at the end of each sophomore year. These were visual evidence of learning A Sense of Place.

Collaborating With Colleagues

Our small school district was proactive as far as keeping up with educational trends. In-services trained us in the Madeline Hunter method of classroom management and we were encouraged to apply many of her principles into our teaching. Other in-services introduced the faculty to collaboration and we were given some time during our in-services to work with colleagues and to brainstorm ways to teach units together. In true rural fashion, however, this work was encouraged and not demanded. Teachers in our district were all given a great deal of independence in choosing the work of their classes. Many chose to use textbooks and prepared materials. Others were more willing to try new approaches. The most successful and extensive collaboration that I did was the collaboration with the Biology teacher. Actually, the first teacher left and a young teacher, a graduate of our school and a former student, was hired to be the secondary science department. Together we taught students about a native prairie, wetlands, and the Platte River Valley. History, Language Arts, and Biology came together in what seemed to be a logical blending of content material. As an English teacher, I found that the students' writings about the prairie and the cranes were enriched by the material they learned in science class before we took them on the field trips.

A second very successful collaboration came about when a new, young art teacher came to teach in our school. After one of our in-services about collaboration, he and I brainstormed a curriculum that combined art and speech for the eighth graders. He found ways to add art to every speech that we did and the kids loved making art for visual aids for their speeches. We went outside to sketch in the style of plains artist Keith Jacobshagen, researched in the library about classic artists, and wrote an informative speech that incorporated student art in the style of that artist. One of the most important concepts that emerged from this work was an awareness of the universality of art. Students studied classic artists as well as a contemporary artist who painted a familiar Nebraska landscape. Both styles were reflected in the artwork that they constructed. Connecting rural life with classical art occurred almost seamlessly. The kids learned so much about artists and used their own creativity for the art projects. Mr. Smith and I discovered that we had completely opposite teaching styles but with some give and take on both sides, we created a class that met the objectives of both of our content areas.

Another collaboration involved the seniors. My senior English class was in a kind of flux. I used some traditional British literature but also incorporated American and World Literature novels. Again, I had administrative and community support for this changing curriculum; no one insisted that the senior year be exclusively British literature. After an in-service on collaboration, the senior history teacher and I decided to teach a long unit together on the history of Civil Rights in the United States. This fit with his curriculum in American Government. I ordered some wonderful free materials from the Teaching Tolerance organization (www.teachingtolerance.org). The students wrote research papers that served as a grade for both classes and it was great to have a longer period of time to show videos since we could combine two class periods when we were in 'collaboration mode.' I believe that the work of these two classes was important for seniors who would soon be leaving the protected environment of a small community. In many ways, it was a reflection of that truism that one should 'think globally, and act locally.'

Although the administration often scheduled some of our in-service time for collaboration, the setting of our small school lent itself to brainstorming. Our school building houses grades K-12; the east wing is the elementary school, and grades 7–12 are in the west wing; the middle offers shared spaces of administrative offices, gyms, the theater, and the cafeteria. Faculties from both wings met often throughout the day: at lunch, in the office running off copies, in the faculty lounge. These meetings often led to conversations that grew into collaborations, some that became 'institutionalized' and others that lasted for only a time. For example, one year I had a study hall of senior and junior high students who had too much time on their hands. The first grade teacher had mentioned at lunch that she had students who needed to practice their reading skills.

I asked my study hall kids if they'd like to be reading pals for the little kids; they voted a resounding yes. Twice a week, the first graders walked down to my classroom and interacted with the 'big kids.' Everyone loved the experience! Another year, I had a creative and smart eighth grade Reading Class that came up with the idea of being pen pals with an elementary class; when I brought this up at lunch one day, the third grade teacher was enthusiastic. Both groups practiced their writing skills.

Beyond the Classroom

Two of these collaborations and my sophomore curriculum of Nebraska Literature led to what would be for me some of the most important and rewarding professional opportunities in my teaching career. First, the Civil Rights Unit allowed our school and senior class to be chosen to participate in a program through the University of Nebraska–Lincoln. A national grant created the Artist's Diversity Program, bringing ethnic artists in different genres to work with college students; a few high schools across the state were chosen to participate as well, all larger schools with diverse ethnic populations. Our school was small and white but the students were open to experiences that they knew they would encounter when they left this place to attend college. The artists who visited the classroom reflected the immigrant influence in our nation: a Conjunto musician from Texas; a Chinese-American artist and poet from San Francisco; a Native American artist from Nebraska; a Jewish playwright and actor from New York. These were important and eye-opening experiences for rural kids from a small town! I was disappointed when budget cuts at the University eventually eliminated the program.

The most far-reaching collaboration for me professionally began in 1997, when the Annenberg Foundation donated a large sum of money to improve education in the United States; thanks to the intervention of some rural education leaders, a small amount of that money was given to rural schools, called the Annenberg Challenge. The National Writing Project used some of the grant money to establish an initiative called Rural Voices, Country Schools. The goal of this program was ". . . to capture, in teacher research, what's good about rural teaching. We are highly aware of the advantages of teaching in rural communities, especially the greater autonomy we have as teachers" (Brooke, 2003, pp. ix–x). At last I was given a formal definition to describe the curriculum I had devised for my sophomore English class: *Place-Conscious Education*.

Robert Brooke, Director of the Nebraska Writing Project, defines Place-Conscious Education as based on the work of Paul Theobald, who "wants an education that immerses learners into the life of human communities *while they are still in school*" (emphasis in original; quoted in Brooke, 2003, p. 6). Brooke notes that Place-Conscious education ". . . isn't in any way a parochial education . . . it begins with students' real civic efficacy in their local place and extends outward" (2003, p. 7). Brooke chose eight rural teachers to be part of Nebraska's Rural Voices, Country School's team and I was one of those teachers. We flew to northern California that summer and met the other teams from Washington, Pennsylvania, Louisiana, and Arizona. Here we shared the work of our rural schools. Suddenly the prose, poetry, and photography of place compiled by my sophomores had an audience beyond our community and state. In Nebraska, our team met often during the school year. Our task was to bring the summer institute, a staple of the program of the Nebraska Writing Project and always held on a college campus, out to a rural school. My school was chosen for the very first Rural Writing Institute. Twenty teachers from across rural Nebraska met in Henderson for a three-week institute; we ate ethnic foods, went on field trips to the preserved prairie, a pioneer cemetery, and the Blue River. As teachers immersed themselves into this local culture and geography, we also wrote about our own places: our childhood memories and our present classrooms and communities. Even though that first rural writing institute was experimental in many ways, we created a model that has been used almost every summer since. I have co-facilitated 10 rural writing institutes across Nebraska and the model fits our rural schools well. Nebraska has many small schools spread out in locations that can be isolating for teachers. At the institutes, rural teachers form partnerships with other teachers that last long beyond the summer.

The second task that the Nebraska RV, CS team took on was the writing of a book that described the work of the Nebraska Writing Project in our state. Each teacher on the team wrote a chapter and we met often to critique one another's writing and to offer feedback. My chapter was called, appropriately, "A Sense of Place." In 2003, our book, *Rural Voices: Place-Conscious Education and the Teaching of Writing*, edited by Robert Brooke, was published by Teachers College Press and the National Writing Project. We were very proud of this accomplishment! Our work now had a national audience.

At the same time, my school became part of the Annenberg Challenge by participating in an initiative called School at the Center. Each participating school and community had to create a committee made up of members from both the rural community and the school. We met often with other towns in our region of the state. At these meetings, the work that was done in each place was shared and we learned from one another. We were guided in this work by Dr. Paul Olson and others from the University of Nebraska. Dr. Olson often reminded us that our goal was to teach young people how to make both a life and a living in a rural place. Place! That word was to figure prominently in my life and in the professional work that I was now engaged in. I was secretly proud that I had included that word in the curriculum I had created on my own. In 1998, the School at the Center sent me to Bordeaux, France, to present at an international conference; my session shared the work of my students, their poetry, and their photography, with an audience from across the world.

Another benefit that was offered by the School at the Center was training in the Foxfire methodology. This work was begun in Georgia and was prominent in the South but it was new to Nebraska. Foxfire trainers journeyed to Nebraska and a large group of rural teachers met for an intense week of training that pushed our boundaries into ways to teach local place. I was fortunate to also be chosen to work with a group of Atlanta-area teachers who developed curricula that served both urban and rural areas. These were times of learning for me and I incorporated some of the Foxfire ideas into my own classroom, specifically giving students more autonomy in choices. The biggest classroom management changes that I ever made were a result of the Foxfire philosophy: (1) choosing audiences beyond the classroom for student work; and (2) giving students choices over due dates for assignments. Those may seem very simple but it took some of the stress out of teaching when I asked students to construct calendars with due dates for papers and reading. When students knew that their work would have an audience beyond the classroom, they became more careful editors of that work.

My involvement in this work brought personal rewards as well. I have attended 12 national conferences where I both shared my work and learned from others. My work has been recognized with some awards and I have had an article published in *English Journal*.

Rural Realities

Despite the fact that rural schools in Nebraska had good academic reputations, the reality of dwindling populations in the many small towns across the state began to affect local schools, literally the centers of cultural life in these small towns. Mergers began to be the norm for these small towns and new school names for the collaborations appeared. Our own community merged with a smaller school about 11 miles away. It was not easy. Despite intensive and extensive meetings and preparations, squabbles over a new school name, mascot, and school colors brought some stress to both towns. Those first years transported students and faculty alike from town to town as both sites were used; eventually we all learned to adjust and now the entire student body attends school in Henderson.

An unfortunate result of this merger meant that some faculty lost their jobs. The art teacher with whom I had developed such a great combined class was replaced by the art teacher from 'the other school' who had more seniority. After a long, rancorous litigation, the senior history teacher lost his job to the teacher from Bradshaw. Neither of these new staff members was interested in curriculum collaboration; I was saddened to lose the cooperative teaching in those areas. Now I also had to incorporate the history of a new community into my place-based class; as I learned about a new community, my students learned from one another.

Conclusion

The above paragraphs are a small view of 32 years in the same classroom, in the same school, in the same town. I am grateful that I was given the freedom and latitude to create the important work that was done over those 32 years. Of course, my class designs had to meet the criteria of 'academic vigor.' If my students had not learned the essential skills of critical reading, writing, and thinking, the most imaginative assignments would not have been tolerated. If my Speech students had not learned how to write and deliver a variety of speeches, an administrator would have ordered a set of textbooks in the bat of an eye—and directed me to use them. As a professional, these are my responsibilities. But oh how much more enjoyable my teaching was when I knew that I could be the decision-maker and creator of curriculum. In a new book of teacher stories, *What Teaching Means: Stories from American's Classrooms*, coeditor Dan Boster writes in the Preface:

> I wanted to be a teacher because I thought teachers seemed really cool and happy. I remember watching them talk and laugh in the hallways of my high school and how some of them would get these faraway stares while explaining *Hamlet*, Manifest Destiny, or polynomials. I thrived when I was around people who clearly loved what they were talking about and cared deeply about sharing that passion with their students.
>
> (Boster and Valerio, 2012, pp. xi–xii)

I think most teachers love their jobs and the content areas that they teach, but given the freedom to create curricula adds a dimension to the job; perhaps it is the highest compliment of being a professional educator. Can it happen in larger schools? I am sure it can but my experience has been in one small, rural school. I think that my career echoes the rather slick bumper sticker that reflects that parents, and perhaps schools, must give their children both roots and wings. My entire professional experience was rooted in this one small school, in the same classroom, and yet, I was able to travel to places, both physical and metaphorical, beyond that classroom that I could never have imagined. The curricula I created bore the imprint of my voice and created a tradition of excellence that will continue past my presence in the classroom. I am grateful that I was given the opportunity to use that voice.

References

Boster, D., & Valerio, M. (Eds.). (2012). *What teaching means: Stories from American's classrooms.* Omaha, NE: Rogue Faculty Press.

Brooke, R. (Ed.). (2003). *Rural voices: Place-conscious education and the teaching of writing.* New York, NY: Teachers College Press and Berkeley, CA: National Writing Project.

Sebranek, P., Kemper, D., & Meyer, V. (2001). *Writers Inc.* Wilmington, MA: GreatSource Education Group.

CONTRIBUTORS

Sharon Bishop, Heartland Community School, Henderson, Nebraska
Sharon Bishop is a retired high school Language Arts teacher from Henderson, NE, where she taught for 32 years. She is a former codirector of the Nebraska Writing Project and is still a member of that Advisory Board as well as a member of the Board for the NE Center for the Book. Sharon's teaching reflected Place-Conscious Reading and Writing and because of that emphasis, her work has been published in *English Journal* and in *Rural Voices: Place Conscious Education and the Teaching of Writing* (edited by R. Brooke, 2003). She has presented at several national conferences and has co-facilitated many Rural Writing Institutes in rural schools across Nebraska. She was the recipient of the 2006 NCTE/Nebraska High School Teacher of Excellence Award and in 2012 she was inducted into the Nebraska Language Arts Educator's Hall of Fame.

Govinda Budrow, Nay Ah Shing School, Mille Lacs Band of Ojibwe Reservation, Onamia, Minnesota
Govinda Budrow is an elementary teacher at Nay Ah Shing Abinoojiiyag on Mille Lacs reservation in Minnesota. She is licensed in elementary education, Ojibwe language and culture, emotional behavior disorders, and learning disabilities. She is a mother of four children, two born to her and two born of her heart. She is Ojibwe and has focused her personal, professional, and research interest on traditional Ojibwe practices and enhancing opportunities for youth.

Hali Kirby-Ertel, Gardiner High School, Gardiner, Montana
Hali Kirby is a high school English teacher at Gardiner Public Schools, where she teaches a range of classes: tenth grade English, eleventh grade English, AP

Composition, Creative Writing, Speech & Drama, and Yearbook. She is the codirector of the Yellowstone Writing Project.

Kendra McPheeters-Neal, Lowell High School, Lowell Indiana

Kendra McPheeters-Neal is an English teacher and building literacy coach at Lowell High School in Lowell, Indiana. LHS is the second rural school in which she has taught; she began her career at North Vermillion Junior-Senior High School in Cayuga, Indiana. A teacher since the fall of 2010, she has taught a range of ability levels spanning eighth to twelfth grade, and her concentrations have been primarily in remediating literacy skills in below-grade-level students and in providing coaching supports for instructors looking to incorporate and scaffold reading, writing, and critical thinking in the classroom. In addition to her literacy focus, Mrs. McPheeters-Neal is a New Tech Network–certified teacher with a strong interest in project-based learning instruction and certified Critical Friends Group coach through the National School Reform Faculty.

Roger Nieboer, Nay Ah Shing School, Mille Lacs Band of Ojibwe Reservation, Onamia, Minnesota

Roger Nieboer has worked in tribal schools since 1997. Previously he taught playwriting at the University of California–Davis and the University of California–San Diego and served as a Visiting Professor of English at NKJO, a teachers training college in Bydgoszcz, Poland. Currently he resides on a 99-acre compound in rural Minnesota where he conducts experiments in organic horticulture, avant-garde landscaping, and restorative forestry. In his spare time he collects cultural artifacts (i.e., junk).

Taylor Norman, Purdue University, Department of Curriculum and Instruction, West Lafayette, Indiana

Taylor Norman taught English for five years at McCutcheon High School in Lafayette, Indiana, and is currently a doctoral candidate in English Education at Purdue University. Working primarily with narrative research, Taylor's research interests center largely around the collection and representation of stories told by teachers. Specifically, stories of their experience while working with students and content in today's public school system. Because of Taylor's experience as a high school English teacher as well as an undergraduate instructor in Purdue's teacher education program, inquiries of teacher identity and its influence on teacher experience are elements within her research as well.

Bambi O'Hern, Nay Ah Shing School, Mille Lacs Band of Ojibwe Reservation, Onamia, Minnesota

Bambi Cardias-O'Hern is the fifth grade teacher at Nah Ah Shing Lower School in Mille Lacs Minnesota. She has four years of experience teaching children on the

Mille Lacs Band of Ojibwe Reservation; her teaching experience also includes 19 years teaching in the California and Minnesota Public School Systems. Bambi holds a Bachelor's Degree in Child Development and a Master's Degree in Educational Leadership.

Chea Parton, Purdue University, Department of Curriculum and Instruction, West Lafayette, Indiana

Chea Parton taught at Southern Wells Jr./Sr. High School in Poneto, Indiana, for three years and she is currently a graduate student at Purdue University where she teaches literacy theory for content area teachers. Her research interests include exploring teacher, student, and adolescent as cultural constructs as well as how they affect each other in the classroom.

Kari Patterson, Fairfield High School, Fairfield, Montana

Kari Patterson teaches sophomore and senior English, Honors English, Title English, and Communication Arts at Fairfield High School in Fairfield, Montana. She previously taught middle school in Fort Shaw and Sun River. For eight years, she coordinated gifted & talented and career shadowing programs for five rural schools. She also taught writing for a rural adult education program for eight years.

Jeffrey B. Ross, Belt High School, Belt, Montana

Jeff Ross is beginning his seventh year teaching high school English, Creative Writing, and Drama at Belt High School in Belt, Montana. He holds an M.F.A. in Creative Writing and an M.A. in English Teaching from the University of Montana. He has participated in the Teaching Shakespeare through Performance residency at Shakespeare's Globe in London, the Yellowstone Writing Project (NWP), and has presented at state, national, and international conferences.

Leslie Susan Rush, University of Wyoming, Laramie, Wyoming

Leslie S. Rush is professor in the Department of Secondary Education and Associate Dean for Undergraduate Programs in the College of Education at the University of Wyoming, in Laramie, Wyoming. As an English teacher educator and a researcher in adolescent literacy and teacher professional development, Dr. Rush has been an active member of the National Council of Teachers of English and its affiliate, the Council on English Education, throughout her career. She was named the coeditor of the journal of CEE, *English Education*, in 2009, and is now finishing a five-year term as editor. Her research agenda includes instructional coaching in middle and high school settings, creative and multigenre writing instruction, multiliteracies and multimodality, and critical literacy and comprehension instruction. Dr. Rush is also a member of a national research team examining the content, position, and makeup of English pedagogy coursework in university-based English teacher education programs.

Gregg Rutter, Nay Ah Shing School, Mille Lacs Band of Ojibwe Reservation, Onamia, Minnesota
Gregg Rutter is the Gifted and Talented Education coordinator at Nay Ah Shing School on the Mille Lacs Band of Ojibwe reservation in Minnesota. He worked as a classroom teacher and gifted student cluster teacher at suburban Minneapolis schools before his work at Nay Ah Shing. Gregg earned his Master of Arts in Teaching degree at the University of St. Thomas and has continued his studies at Hamline University focusing on Gifted Education. He earned his undergraduate degree in Architecture from the University of Minnesota and also studied poetics at Naropa University in Colorado.

Jeff Spanke, Purdue University, Department of Curriculum and Instruction, West Lafayette, Indiana
Jeff Spanke is a former high school English teacher and current doctoral candidate in English Education at Purdue University. His literary passions include nineteenth-century American Literature and post-WWII fiction. His research interests involve adolescent writing instruction, alternative schooling, and service learning. For his views on rural education, Jeff will forever be indebted to the Charging Chargers of North Montgomery High School.

INDEX

focus of 37; involvement in classroom planning 24–5; misconceptions of 57; needs of 116, 118; as Other 34, 46; queer 28, 31; relationship with teachers 16, 32, 55, 59, 63, 68, 107–110; special needs 1, 122; teacher connections with 76; tolerance of gender and sexuality by 27–30; transgender 26–7
subjectivities: conflicting 6; suburban 19–22, 30–1, 36

Teach Like A Champion (Lemov) 64
teacher identity development 8, 14
teacher preparation 4, 7, 48; socially just 6–8
teachers: advice to new teachers 50; agendas of 112; autobiography of 15; challenges of 13, 50–3, 62–3, 65–7; effect of students on 32; emotional meltdown 66–7; experience of 134–5; experienced 73–7; influence of 110–112; interviewing for jobs 48–9, 59, 106; mental challenges of 44–5; as outsiders 4, 42, 96; pre-service 7, 48; as public intellectuals 5–6, 77; relationships with parents 42, 59, 63; relationships with students 16, 32, 55, 59, 63, 68, 107–110; resiliency of 75–6; responsibility of 64–5, 109–112; stereotypes of 45; as strangers 20–5, 31; *see also* burnout; identity
teaching *see* education

teaching organizations 7
"Teaching Shakespeare through Performance" 74
Teaching Tolerance organization 130
Teaching Writing as Reflective Practice (Hillocks) 87
tests, high-stakes *see* standardized testing
Theobald, Paul 132
The Things They Carried (O'Brien) 112
Thoreau, Henry David 40, 46, 47
time, differing concepts of 116–18, 120–2
To Kill a Mockingbird (Lee) 104
tracking 101
transsexuality 26–7, 62

Umphrey, Michael 88, 92
urban education 5, 31

values: of community 22, 95, 97–8; conflicting 23; social 112; of students and families 96–7; *see also* culture
Van Wyhe, Tamara 79

Walden (Thoreau) 40, 46, 47
What Teaching Means: Stories from America's Classrooms (ed. Boster and Valerio) 134
"'Who Makes Much of A Miracle?' The Evolution of a School's Poetic Culture" (Strever) 79
"Wisdom Sits in Places" (Basso) 88
writing: assignments 99–100; vulnerable 34